FRIVOLITY UNBOUND

FRIVOLITY UNBOUND

Six Masters of the Camp Novel

Thomas Love Peacock
Max Beerbohm
Ronald Firbank
E. F. Benson
P. G. Wodehouse
Ivy Compton-Burnett

by Robert F. Kiernan

A Frederick Ungar Book
CONTINUUM • NEW YORK

1990

The Continuum Publishing Company
370 Lexington Avenue
New York, NY 10017

Printed in the United States of America

Library of Congress Cataloging-in-Publication Data

Kiernan, Robert F.
Frivolity unbound : six masters of the camp novel, Thomas Love Peacock, Max Beerbohm, Ronald Firbank, E. F. Benson, P. G. Wodehouse, Ivy Compton-Burnett / by Robert F. Kiernan.
p. cm. — (Literature and life series)
"A Frederick Ungar book."
Includes bibliographical references.
ISBN 0-8264-0465-0
1. English fiction—20th century—History and criticism. 2. Humorous stories, English—History and criticism. 3. Peacock, Thomas Love, 1785–1866—Criticism and interpretation. I. Title. II. Series.
PR888.H85K5 1990
823′.9120917—dc20 89-49041
CIP

It is so easy to be solemn;
it is so hard to be frivolous.

—Chesterton

Contents

Acknowledgments

For their many kindnesses, I am grateful to librarians at the British Library, the New York Public Library, and the Manhattan College Library—most notably to Geoff Adams; Dominick Caldiero; Gloria Degnan, SC; Máire Duchon; Greg Hauptman; Thomas O'Connor, FSC; Adele Reardon; Kate Shanley; and Brian Trainor. It is a pleasure once again to acknowledge Evander Lomke, my editor at Continuum, whose support of this project was unstinting; Professor Ernest Speranza, who graciously helped with the galley proofs; also to thank Manhattan College and Professor Walter G. Emge, provost, for a sabbatical leave during which most of the book was written.

Acknowledgments

1

The Camp Enterprise

Among the ne plus ultras dear to the camp sensibility is the Royal Pavilion in Brighton, England. A bizarre, pseudo-Indian fantasy of bulbous domes, tent-shaped roofs, and latticed verandas, it was evolved in the years 1787–1822 from a neoclassic structure and employed briefly as a summer palace by the prince regent, later to be George IV, to whose enthusiasm for the architectural flourish it stands monument. Indeed, the pavilion's heady aesthetic of the exaggerated, the theatrical, the passionate, and the naive almost defines camp taste. The Tiffany lamp that mimics a wisteria vine, most cinema posters from the 1940s and 1950s, Liberace's feather-and-leather wardrobe, and Jimmy Carter's famous adventure with a killer-rabbit might all be analyzed as camp phenomena in exactly such terms.

Less well known than the Royal Pavilion but equally felicitous as camp was George IV's coronation in 1820. In the wake of unsuccessful divorce proceedings against his spouse, the king was determined that Queen Caroline should not enter Westminster Abbey with him and be crowned, although she had every constitutional right. His troops prevented the queen's attendance at the coronation ceremony, but the king was then faced with a public procession to Westminster Hall, during which he was expected to walk under a canopy borne by the barons of the Cinque Ports. The day happened to be very hot; the king, to be very fat; and the baron on the king's right was therefore burdened not only with a canopy pole but with an embroidered bag full of handkerchiefs for the royal brow. The baron could only pass a handkerchief to the greatly perspiring monarch by taking one hand from his pole, an action that caused the canopy to wobble alarmingly. Probably recalling that a collapsed canopy had completely engulfed James II when Samuel Pepys was one of the honorary barons, the king lumbered out from under the dubious protection of the canopy and tried to outpace his elderly attendants. What could the barons do but abide by their sworn duty? Not concerned that the king might be snared as in a net for the pursuant queen, they shuffled faster with the lurching canopy, so many entomologists in pursuit of an excessively alarmed butterfly. The king waddled faster still, straight into the annals of camp.

Such instances of camp proliferate in all forms of art and behavior that offer the opportunity for a contrast between negligible content and elaborate form. One thinks of the patter songs of Flanders and Swann, for instance, but not the scat of jazz singers; the ostentatious mausoleums spaced like tourist cabins in New York City's Woodlawn Cemetery, but not the minimalist Vietnam Memorial in Washington; the bitchy bon mots of Truman Capote, but not the wisecracks of Dorothy Parker. Follies, those eccentric and generally useless erections that satisfied a landscaping whim of the eighteenth century, are almost always camp—sufficiently so to merit the anciently Anglo-Saxon, contemporaneously camp exclamations "Coo!" and "Cor!" None of Henry James's novels but virtually all of his recorded conversations are camp. Edith Wharton's account of James's asking an old man directions to the King's Road is classic:

> "My good man, if you'll be good enough to come here, please; a little nearer—so," and as the old man came up: "My friend, to put it to you in two words, this lady and I have just arrived here from *Slough;* that is to say, to be more strictly accurate, we have recently *passed through* Slough on our way here, having actually motored to Windsor from Rye, which was our point of departure; and the darkness having overtaken us, we should be much obliged if you would tell us where we now are in relation, say, to the High Street, which, as you of course know, leads to the Castle, after leaving on the left hand the turn down to the railway station."
>
> I was not surprised to have this extraordinary appeal met by silence, and a dazed expression on the old wrinkled face at the window; nor to have James go on: "In short" (his invariable prelude to a fresh series of explanatory ramifications), "in short, my good man, what I want to put to you in a word is this: supposing we have already (as I have reason to think we have) driven past the turn down to the railway station (which, in that case, by the way, would probably not have been on our left hand, but on our right), where are we now in relation to . . ."
>
> "Oh, please," I interrupted, feeling myself utterly unable to sit through another parenthesis, "do ask him where the King's Road is."
>
> "Ah—? The King's Road? Just so! Quite right! Can you, as a matter

of fact, my good man, tell us where, in relation to our present position, the King's Road exactly *is?*"[1]

To recognize such examples of camp in artifacts and in human behavior is relatively easy, but to define the nature and psychological terrain of camp is more difficult. The word itself is fraught with difficulties, for its origin is obscure, its usage somewhat cultish, its spawn of grammatically cognate forms like *camping* and *to camp* a labyrinth. That the original, adjectival form is a Victorian coinage seems likely on the basis of its first recording in a 1909 book of words, J. Redding Ware's *Passing English of the Victorian Era,* wherein it is applied to "actions and gestures of exaggerated emphasis" and thought to be a derivation from French. *Used chiefly by persons of exceptional want of character,* Ware warns severely.[2] By the 1920s the term was slanted to effeminate homosexual actions, at least in theatrical and Hollywood argot, but it retained its more general application to actions and gestures of exaggerated emphasis. The verbal forms of the word ("to camp," "to camp it up," "camping") seem to have emerged in the 1930s and to have led in turn to a noun form for both the doer and the action ("he's a Camp," "on a camp"), sometimes capitalized, in the 1940s. The word retains today both its general and its homosexual applications.[3]

Interest in camp as a cultural phenomenon began to appear in the 1950s, most notably in a distinction between high and low camp articulated by the novelist Christopher Isherwood in *The World in the Evening.* In response to the question "Did you ever run across the word 'camp'?" Isherwood writes:

You thought it meant a swishy little boy with peroxided hair, dressed in a picture hat and a feather boa, pretending to be Marlene Dietrich? Yes, in queer circles, they call *that* camping. It's all very well in its place, but it's an utterly debased form. . . . What I mean by camp is something much more fundamental. You can call the other Low Camp, if you like; then what I'm talking about is High Camp. High Camp is the whole emotional basis of the ballet, for example, and of course of baroque art. You see, true High Camp always has an underlying seriousness. You can't camp about something you don't take seriously. You're not making fun of it; you're making fun out of it. You're expressing what's basically serious to you in terms of fun and artifice and elegance. Baroque art is largely camp about religion. The ballet is camp about love.[4]

Complaining that camp is "terribly hard to define," Isherwood resorts to illustrations. Mozart is camp, he says; Beethoven, not; El Greco and Dostoyevski are camp; Rembrandt and Flaubert, not. Dostoyevski, he claims, is "the founder of the whole school of modern Psycho-Camp which was later developed by Freud."[5]

Isherwood's effort to define camp through illustrations rather than through extended analysis led to Susan Sontag's influential essay of 1964 "Notes on 'Camp.'" In her stated conviction that the fugitive sensibility of camp makes jottings more appropriate than argument, the author provides a list of illustrations similar to Isherwood's and makes a series of random observations. Camp is both a way of looking at things and a quality that can be discovered in objects and in the behavior of persons, she stipulates. It is a "love of the exaggerated, the 'off,' of things-being-what-they-are-not" that responds in a particular way both to the markedly attenuated and to the strongly exaggerated.[6] It responds on the one hand to the androgynous Greta Garbo, Sontag says, and on the other hand to such stylists of the exaggerated temperament as Bette Davis, Barbara Stanwyck, and Tallulah Bankhead. Max Beerbohm's *Zuleika Dobson, Swan Lake,* the *Enquirer* tabloid of the 1960s (both its headlines and its stories), Aubrey Beardsley drawings, Vincenzo Bellini's operas, old Flash Gordon comic books, the novels of Ronald Firbank and Ivy Compton-Burnett—all, she says, are camp.

Without reference to Isherwood's distinction between high and low camp, Sontag suggests a distinction between naive and deliberate varieties of the genre. "Pure Camp," she insists, "is always naïve."[7] Like Isherwood's, her distinction is implicitly hierarchical: "Camp which knows itself to be Camp ('camping') is usually less satisfying," she says.[8] Reflecting an immediate confusion of Isherwood's distinction with Sontag's, the *Random House Dictionary* in 1966 defined *high camp* as "an ironic or amusing quality present in an extravagant gesture, style, or form . . . *when the inappropriate relationship is used self-consciously.*" *Low camp* it defined as ". . . *when used unself-consciously, unknowledgeably,* or *inadequately*" [emphasis mine].[9] This clumsy amalgam had the effect of muddying both Isherwood's and Sontag's waters, rendering the terms *high* and *low camp* inconsistent in general usage. Without reference to high and low, the *Random House Dictionary* now defines camp as "something that provides sophisticated, knowing amusement, as by virtue of its being artlessly mannered or stylized, self-consciously artificial and extravagant, or teasingly ingenuous and sentimental."[10]

Sontag's essay has been particularly influential in laying out a history of camp with its roots in the Enlightenment:

> The soundest starting point seems to be the late 17th and early 18th century, because of that period's extraordinary feeling for artifice, for surface, for symmetry; its taste for the picturesque and the thrilling, its elegant conventions for representing instant feeling and the total presence of character—the epigram and the rhymed couplet (in words), the flourish (in gesture and music). The late 17th and early 18th century is the great period of Camp: Pope, Congreve, Walpole, etc., but not Swift; *les précieux* in France; the rococo churches of Munich; Pergolesi. Somewhat later: much of Mozart. But in the 19th century, what had been distributed throughout all of high culture now becomes a special taste; it takes on overtones of the acute, the esoteric, the perverse. Confining the story to England alone, we see Camp continuing wanly through 19th century aestheticism (Burne-Jones, Pater, Ruskin, Tennyson), emerging full-blown with the Art Nouveau movement in the visual and decorative arts, and finding its conscious ideologists in such "wits" as Wilde and Firbank.[11]

One might object that in the secular, tolerant mood of the Enlightenment human beings were thought naturally good and to find their greatest happiness in the exercise of benevolence. Camp tends to celebrate the opposite: human beings caught up in the lesser iniquities, who find their greatest happiness in vaunts of egotism. Camp would seem to that extent an antiestablishment humor. Such is the position of the sociologist Esther Newton, who grants camp an exclusively homosexual provenance and argues in her study of female impersonators that it is "strategy for a situation."[12] The situation she perceives is that the great majority of homosexuals must suppress their real selves in favor of speciously heterosexual selves in order to gain establishment respectability. Their compensating strategy, she argues, is a humor that reduces the established male/female categories to mere roles, exaggerated and consciously stagy. "Camp is suffused with the perception of 'being as playing a role' and 'life as theatre,'" she says, quoting Sontag.[13] The film critic Parker Tyler made essentially the same point when he observed of the high camp performances of Garbo, "How resplendent seems the art of acting! It is all *impersonation,* whether the sex underneath is true or not."[14] The largely homosexual audiences that attended Judy Garland's last concerts might be said to have had a similar enthusiasm for life as theater.

But is this psychosexual mode of understanding necessary to establish Garbo's, Garland's, or any other performances as camp? A proprietary attitude in the homosexual subculture resents any effort to edit homosexuality out of the genre, but there is a broader human context in which excessive stylization of whatever kind is camp, from Garbo's androgynous sexuality, to the Royal Pavilion at Brighton, to the Old Pretender's workaday discourse. Problems inherent in the exclusively psychosexual point of view are considerable. In terms of "strategy for a situation," for instance, what is one to make of the streak of cruelty in the homosexual audiences' response to the Garland concerts, memorialized in Peter Allen's admonitory song "That's a Lady up There"? Comically speaking, what is one to make of the destructive self-contempt that such a streak of cruelty implies?

It strains the nature of camp, it seems to me, to perceive it as anti-anything. If there is a camp spectrum of humor, it shades only at its edges into the oppositional stances of satire and parody. Its central note is celebration, a shameless love of all that is exaggerated, not just the gender-exaggerated. Indeed, shamelessness is of its essence, for what camp has historically afforded its audiences—its artists, too—is an alternative to the morally correct laughter of satire, parody, and all other shame-begetting forms of humor. Camp invites a sophisticated, amoral mode of laughter that recognizes it might be critical but elects to be uncritically affectionate, not in a spirit of perversity, but for the psychic relief that such amorality and such release of affection afford.

The attitude of E. F. Benson toward the novelist Marie Corelli illumines this amoral affection as a necessary disposition of camp artists and their audiences. In his memoir *Final Edition,* Benson writes with fond amusement of Corelli, noting her absurdly stylized devotion to Ye Olde England, her belief that she was showing him a famous Canaletto when she was showing him actually a portrait by Frans Hals, and her inane baby talk ("Now ickle droppie more . . .") as she thrust upon an exhausted guest a teaspoon of warm brandy and water. On the basis of such anecdotes, Benson's readers will recognize immediately that Corelli was a prototype for Lucia of Riseholme, Benson's most successful character and the eponymous heroine of *Queen Lucia, Lucia in London,* and other novels. Yet of Corelli Benson writes, "In a work of fiction a character like hers would appear preposterous; the least critical readers would reject it as fantastically unreal."[15] Does it require, then, a totally *un*critical reader *not* to reject the fantastical Lucia while recognizing and applauding her outrageousness? Does it require the camp sensibility, perforce, for author and readers alike to see in Lucia one of the great stylists of camp temperament—the equal of a Bette Davis, an Edith Sitwell, a Lady Bracknell? Indeed, to see in Lucia a shining tribute to Corelli? "Small beer with a head on it," Benson once described the *Lucia* novels.[16] One could do worse for a definition of camp.

One could also do better, of course. Camp is difficult to define apart from such whimsies of metaphor because it depends crucially upon a style of appreciation as well as upon the structure of incongruities that informs all comedy. This is why the seriousness of one generation or stratum of society can be perceived as campiness by another. At the coronation of George IV, alluded to earlier, neither the king nor his honorary barons were consciously camping, and contemporary witnesses of the event murmured only of lese majesty. What makes the incident funny is its play of incongruities—petulancy in high places, a ceremonious procession become farcical, the mutinous king and the insistently dutiful barons—but to be appreciable specifically as camp those incongruities must be held in awareness by a style of mind that cherishes them with either real or affected naiveté. Camp humor is in this respect insistently frivolous. All other modes of comic response are shadowed with a moral seriousness that would covertly rebuke the monarch for his unkingly panic. In the distinctively camp response, he is admired for his extravagant, quirky humanity with an appreciativeness made easy by moral disencumbrance. Such is the notion of camp I mean to suggest by the title of this study. All other forms of humor are encumbered, even defined by a covert morality; camp is something more free—a frivolity unbound.

Sontag observes in her "Notes on 'Camp'" that "to snare a sensibility in words, especially one that is alive and powerful, one must be tentative and nimble."[17] Having argued that the perception of camp depends not so much upon acumen as upon just such a style of mind, I conceive of this book as a series of appreciations as much as a literary argument. For the same reason—that my mode is appreciation as much as argument—I have tried to suggest the camp appeal of novels like *Nightmare Abbey* and *Zuleika Dob-*

son without arguing the presence of camp humor relentlessly or debating theories of camp at every turn of a paragraph. To the degree that my focus is the tradition of camping in the English novel, I do not mean to suggest that the tradition begins with Peacock and ends with Compton-Burnett, nor that it is limited to the six novelists upon whom I concentrate, nor, even, that there *is* a tradition—but more of that later. I will confess, however, to passing over major writers like Fielding, Sterne, and Joyce (who are arguably camps) in my esteem for those six writers, whose mastery of the camp narrative is less often noted.

Elizabeth Bowen observes rightly that an Edwardian dread of Victorian dowdiness effected a lightening of the English novel in the early 1900s.[18] With the exception of Peacock, who died in 1866, all of my subjects are a part of that lightening—writers for whom the impudence, the involutions, and the elegant eccentricities of Peacock's camping became once again a viable, even necessary stance. Are they as shallow as they are generally thought? So many escapist children? "Their shallowness was a policy, however unconscious," says Bowen. "We owe it to them to see not only the speciousness but the ingenuousness of their contrived illusions." Indeed.

2

The Enlightened Palette: Thomas Love Peacock

As J. B. Priestley has observed, Thomas Love Peacock constitutes a treacherous subject for the literary critic. "He is one of those authors," Priestley asserts, "who, in their wilfulness, eccentricity, originality, leave a very definite impression on the mind, but nevertheless are very difficult to 'place.'"[1] Behind that difficulty for the critic stands an array of paradoxes in the historical man. Grounds are ample for the current view of Peacock as a Tory satirist, deeply conservative in all matters touching social change,[2] yet he was viewed in his own age as politically radical because Tory politicians and policies were favorite targets of his pen. A self-taught classicist who was well versed in the intellectual discourse of the Enlightenment and who was unusually well-read in classical, continental, and English literature, he was at the same time deeply contemptuous of Oxford and its scholars. Although his novels constitute exuberant celebrations of fellowship and conviviality, his reputation in literary history is that of a "disdainful aristocratic amateur of letters" who was irritatingly self-sufficient.[3]

Peacock's friendship with the poet Percy Bysshe Shelley is especially problematic. On the one hand, it gave him credentials as a critic of the romantic personality and of the literature and society of the Romantic Age, and in many ways it gave him intellectual focus. On the other hand, Peacock wrote *Nightmare Abbey,* which is popularly regarded as an attack on Shelley, in the period when he was most engaged with the intellectual circle that gathered around the poet.

Such paradoxes, both real and false, stand behind the elusiveness of tone and theme in Peacock's novels and make possible a range of critical understandings, not the least of them that Peacock was a camp humorist. Peacock himself espoused what might be termed a utilitarian theory of comedy, for he argued that comedy has always the purpose of castigating folly,[4] but one suspects that his theorizing was posterior to a simpler instinct to exercise his wit and make people laugh. Without in any way denigrating the current interest in Peacock as a topical satirist, it remains possible to stand with those readers who value him primarily for his camping.[5] Two of the novels are especially satisfying as instances of camp: the early *Headlong Hall* and the masterful *Nightmare Abbey.*

Headlong Hall (1816)

With *Headlong Hall,* Peacock discovered his novelistic formula. Henry Headlong, Esquire, is as fond of shooting, hunting, and drinking as any other Welsh squire, but he has unaccountably discovered books and longs to be thought a philosopher and man of taste. Accordingly, he sets out to make the acquaintance of such men. Finding none in Oxford, he proceeds to London, where he discovers them in abundance. Nothing will satisfy him but to have his new friends all together to pass their Christmas arguing over old port and Burgundy at his rural seat in Caernarvonshire. The novel begins with the transport of his primary guests in the Holyhead mail coach: Mr. Foster, a perfectibilian who is convinced that the world is steadily improving; Mr. Escot, a deteriorationist who is equally convinced of the world's steady decline; Mr. Jenkison, a statu-quo-ite who believes that in balance everything is much as it was; and the Reverend Doctor Gaster, who is the first of a long line of gourmandizing parsons in Peacock's novels. The four "crocheteers" (as it is customary to term such Pavonine characters) are joined at Headlong Hall by Mr. Cranium, a phrenologist; Mr. Panscope, an insistently transcendental philosopher; and Messrs. Gall, Treacle, MacLaurel, and Nightshade. The first two are professional reviewers and inept poets; the second two, professional poets and inept reviewers. The last arrivals are Mr. Cornelius Chromatic, a "scientific" amateur musician; his daughters, Miss Tenorina and Miss Graziosa; Sir Patrick O'Prism, a dilettante painter; and O'Prism's aunt, Miss Philomela Poppyseed, a popular novelist. Mr. Cranium is accompanied by his daughter, Cephalis. Caprioletta Headlong, the squire's sister, serves as hostess of the gathering. In temporary residence is Marmaduke Milestone, a landscape gardener of considerable fame who hopes that Squire Headlong will commission him to improve the estate.

Once the guests are assembled, Peacock is little interested in plotting a course of action for them. He conveys them from a welcoming dinner to a short round of country-house activities and finally to the Christmas celebration that is the ostensible climax of their visit to Headlong Hall. Conversation, not action, is the donnée of the novel, and incidental developments are only pegs on which to hang ideological disputes. The morning of general departure sees a number of unexpected betrothals, however: Foster to Caprioletta, Headlong to Tenorina, O'Prism to Graziosa, and Escot to Cephalis. The Reverend Doctor Gaster promptly effects the metamorphosis of these eight people into four couples, and the novel ends with the party dispersing amid promises to reassemble in August.

Like all of Peacock's novels, *Headlong Hall* is arguably a roman à clef. The chief crocheteers—Foster the perfectibilian, Escot the deteriorationist, and Jenkison the statu-quo-ite—articulate the positions generally adopted in conversation by Shelley, Peacock, and Thomas Jefferson Hogg, the latter a barrister and litterateur who was a member of Shelley's entourage. The incomprehensibly philosophical Panscope is the first of several Pavonine burlesques of the poet Samuel Taylor Coleridge, and the burlesque is unmistakable, however crude. No single individual is suggested by Cranium, but his interest in phrenology evokes a contemporary vogue for the study that was unexpectedly endorsed by the prestigious *Edinburgh Review,* whose critical hegemony cuts through the world of *Headlong Hall* like an exceedingly blunt knife. The *Review* is almost certainly the publisher of Messrs. Gall (possibly Francis Jeffrey, a founder and editor of the quarterly), MacLaurel (probably the Scots poet Thomas Campbell, but possibly John Wilson, one of the first critics to do justice to Wordsworth's poetry), and Nightshade (almost certainly the poet Robert Southey). Philomela Poppyseed is probably Mrs. Amelia Opie, a minor novelist and poet of the time whose endorsement by the *Review* was a scandal in literary circles. Milestone is based clearly on Humphrey Repton, who succeeded William Kent and Capability Brown as the foremost landscape gardener of his day. O'Prism is Uvedale Price, a leading polemicist against Repton's art.

But such correspondences between fictional and historical persons are of minor interest in *Headlong Hall.* Indeed, Peacock generally eschews any attempt to evoke the particulars of physiognomy, character, or situation that would transform his characters into caricatures of the usual roman à clef sort. Panscope is not a poet and has not Coleridge's opium addiction, which would have been obvious elements for Peacock to introduce had caricature been his impulse, and Foster's marriage to Caprioletta contains no whiff of Shelley's cohabitational confusions, although Peacock disapproved and took Harriet Westbrook's part when the poet left his wife for Mary Godwin in 1814. Instead of such roman à clef correspondences, characters' names carry the burden of their identities. Doctor Gaster must of course be a gourmand; Mr. Cranium, a phrenologist; Mr. Chromatic, a musician; Mr. Panscope, a "chemical, botanical, geological, astronomical, mathematical, metaphysical, meteorological, anatomical, physiological, galvanistical, musical, pictorial, bibliographical, critical philosopher." For the names of his main characters, Peacock is at pains to produce multilingual etymologies that shift the process of discerning their identities away from caricature to a fanciful onomastic system in which Englishmen have names drawn from the classical Greek. In extended footnotes, only partially quoted here, he tells us airily that *Foster* is "quasi Φωστηρ,—from φαος and τηρεω, lucem servo, conservo, observo, custodio"; *Escot,* "quasi ξς σκοτον, *in tenebras,* scilicet, intuens"; *Jenkison,* "derived from αιεν εξ ισων, *semper ex aequalibus*—scilicet, mensuris, omnia metiens."

It would seem, then, that Foster, Escot, and Jenkison only embody positions that Shelley, Peacock, and Hogg took customarily in argument—that they are really nothing more than spokesmen for points of view that interested Peacock independently of the persons who held the views.[6] Partially because of this distancing of ideas from the men who championed them, Peacock cannot be classified as a novelist of ideas in the same sense as William Godwin, H. G. Wells, or Aldous Huxley. He has, moreover, no driving polemic; no need to identify those in ostensible error; not even an impulse to maintain ideological consistency. It might be said that he is a satirist of ideas rather than an ideological satirist, but even that distinction conveys something militant in Peacock's stance that is false to the sensibility informing *Headlong Hall.* Peacock's most distinctive note is his sense of intellectual sport—of argument as reducible to the game called Cross Questions and Crooked Answers. Ideas to him seem indistinguishable from idées fixes, and for that reason the dining table, not the debating hall, is the Pavonine setting of choice. "His mind," says Priestley, "lived in the kingdom of philosophic theories and systems and ideals, and if Shelley was its bard, Peacock was its Court Jester. It is this position, as the comedian of the life of ideas, that makes Peacock a unique figure in English Literature."[7]

The reduction of ideas to idées fixes is the basic joke of *Headlong Hall.* Although Foster, Escot, and Jenkison each profess to have given their general positions much thought, they fall into their positions so inevitably and with such alacrity that spontaneous thought seems not to interest them at all. To that extent they are predictable and classically comic. Upon their first meeting in the Hollyhead mail coach, for instance, they remark roads and railways, canals and tunnels, and each mounts his hobbyhorse with dispatch. To Foster, such modern transportation systems attest the remarkable progress of man toward a state of unlimited perfection; to Escot, they are "links in the great chain of corruption, which will soon fetter the whole human race in irreparable slavery and incurable wretchedness"; to Jenkison, they give evidence of tendencies to moral perfectibility and deterioration in exact balance. Thereafter, the three philosophers marshal the same points of view with metronomic regularity. Roast meat at breakfast inspires a debate upon the eating of animal products, Escot declaring it to be one of the principal causes of mankind's degeneracy, Foster disagreeing, and Jenkison declaring the question "in equipoise." When the three tour their host's estate, the scenery seems improvable to Foster, deteriorated to Escot, and just what it ought to be to Jenkison. Even a decision to join the ladies after a postprandial bottle of Burgundy inspires the familiar viewpoints:

> The little butler now waddled in with a summons from the ladies to tea and coffee. . . . Mr. Escot strenuously urged the necessity of immediate adjournment, observing that the longer they continued drinking the worse they should be. Mr. Foster seconded the motion, declaring the transition from the bottle to female society to be an indisputable amelioration of the state of the sensitive man. Mr. Jenkison allowed the squire and his two brother philosophers to settle the point between them, concluding that he was just as well in one place as another.

This three-way polarization of the philosophers' viewpoints is echoed in other, equally mechanical arrays of opinion and person. The inclusion of a musician, a painter, and a writer among the minor guests seems excessively contrived because nothing much is achieved by their coming together. The three artists never discuss art among themselves in this conversation novel; nor do they debate their artistic proclivities. They are simply addenda to a house party whose guest list is ruled by schematics. In another instance of a contrivance more elaborate than is warranted, the symmetry of Gall's and Treacle's names and of MacLaurel's and Nightshade's names is reinforced by their gratuitous pairing as reviewer-poets and poet-reviewers. Peacock composes a world as formal as an eighteenth-century garden in such respects, but his symmetries creak in a calculated way and his taxonomies are excessively tidy. As much as Milestone's ambition to blast the landscape into submission in the creation of natural effects, Peacock's absolute control of his ostensibly free-spirited characters is a kind of charade. Its effect is not to sharpen the force with which he parodies his philosophers and supporters of ideas but to blunt the cutting edge of that parody with whimsy.

A love story that counterpoints the conversational structure of the novel is particularly successful as a whimsy. Escot and Cephalis are deeply in love when the novel begins, but Cranium promises his daughter's hand in marriage to the odious Panscope when Escot fails to show a proper esteem for phrenology. Escot proceeds in heroic fashion to save Cranium's life, but that counts for nothing in Cranium's excessively cerebral world. Indeed, the older man is won to the cause of true love only when Escot presents him with a moldy skull allegedly that of the ancient king Cadwallader. It is all wonderfully unromantic in one sense, romantic in another, and Cranium's willingness to trade a daughter for a dubiously credentialed skull is underscored by Panscope's cold-blooded declaration in defeat "that the monotonous system of female education brought every individual of the sex to so remarkable an approximation of similarity, that no wise man would suffer himself to be annoyed by a loss so easily repaired." But suddenly romance—or a spirit, at least, of getting romance over and done with—is everywhere. Coincidentally with the betrothal of Escot and Cephalis, Squire Headlong is persuaded of the need to produce an heir, and so he proposes to Tenorina. Foster immediately announces his betrothal to Caprioletta, and O'Prism agrees to marry Graziosa to complete the series. Their foursquare march to the altar constitutes a mockery of the headier flights of the romantic novel, of course, a mockery, too, of Poppyseed's fiction, which has taught young ladies "to consider themselves as a sort of commodity, to be put up at public auction, and knocked down to the highest bidder." But more importantly, it is a narrative throwaway, an impudent wink at romantic fiction. It seems Peacock's whimsy, little more, to allow romance its scatterbrained head among his crocheteers.

Such a whimsical development in the narrative suggests a camp sensibility informing the whole. That understanding is furthered by the overwrought effects associated with camp that are Peacock's especial delight as his perfectibilians and deteriorationists drift into absurdity on a tide of stylistic excesses. He is surely camping when he tells us that "Miss Cephalis blushed like a carnation at the sight of Mr. Escot, and Mr. Escot glowed like a corn-poppy at the sight of Miss Cephalis" as Mr. Cranium "underwent several variations, from the dark red of the piony [sic] to the deep blue of the convolvulus." In a wonderfully absurd phrase, the chaise in which Doctor Gaster arrives at Headlong Hall proves drafty because "the frames and glasses had long since discontinued their ancient familiarity." The reverend doctor receives Headlong's congratulation upon his safe arrival with unconsciously arch assurance "that the congratulation was by no means misapplied." Cranium speaks of the "osteosarchaematosplanchnochondroneuromvelous, or to employ a more intelligible term, osseocarnisanguineovisceri-cartilaginonervomedullary, *campages,* or shell, the body." During a lecture on phrenology, he exhibits the skull of a highwayman who was checked in his career "by means of a certain quality inherent in preparations of hemp." He terms that quality of hemp "suspensiveness." Hyperbole is of a piece with such overwriting, as when a corkscrew put to use at the Christmas festivities is said "to have grown so hot under the influence of perpetual friction that it actually set fire to the cork."

In the same comic spirit, Peacock includes among his minor characters a sexton whose Welsh accent amounts to an inability to pronounce *g, b,* and *d,* for which sounds he substitutes *c, p,* and *t* when they occur in the initial position of a word. The result ("Cot pless your honour, I should n't have thought of meeting any pody here at this time of the morning, except, look you, it was the tevil—who, to pe sure, toes not often come upon consecrated cround") is so handsomely ludicrous that Peacock cannot let the joke rest with the sexton. What matter the passage of centuries? What matter the different conventions of spoken and written language? Cadwallader's seventh-century tomb employs the sexton's nineteenth-century dialect (and anachronistic Gothic lettering) in a camp caution to graverobbers:

He that my pones shall ill pestow
Leek in his cround shall never crow.

Examples of such cavalier developments in the narrative might be cited endlessly. In one of the best, Squire Headlong conceives a deep aversion for water on an occasion when his boat capsizes:

This circumstance alone, of the various disasters that befel him, occasioned him any permanent affliction, and he accordingly noted the day in his pocket book as a *dies nefastus,* with this simple abstract, and brief chronicle of the calamity: *Mem. Swallowed two or three pints of water:* without any notice whatever of the concomitant circumstances. These days, of which there were several, were set apart in Headlong Hall for the purpose of anniversary expiation; and, as often as the day returned on which the squire had swallowed water, he not only made a point of swallowing a treble allowance of wine himself, but imposed a heavy mulct on every one of his servants who should be detected in a state of sobriety after sunset: but their conduct on these occasions was so uniformly exemplary, that no instance of the infliction of the penalty appears on record.

Any kind of incremental pattern inspires Peacock to splendidly absurd effects. He loves the ceremonial, dilatory pacing of such patterns and the occasions their pace affords for stately nonsense:

A tradition [was] handed down in Headlong Hall for some few thousand years, that the founder of the family was preserved in the deluge on the summit of Snowdon, and took the name of Rhaiader, which signifies a *waterfall,* in consequence of his having accompanied the water in its descent or diminution, till he found himself comfortably seated on the rocks of Llanberris. But, in later days, when commercial bagsmen began to scour the country, the ambiguity of the sound induced his descendants to drop the suspicious denomination of *Riders,* and translate the word into English; when, not being well pleased with the sound of the *thing,* they substituted that of the *quality,* and accordingly adopted the name *Headlong,* the appropriate epithet of waterfall.

This joke established, Peacock goes on to invent several choruses of a drinking song based on the family lineage, with *Ap-Pistyll* as a fine accretion. It is often his way to keep a joke humming in this manner, elaborate reiteration and some small development emphasizing the camp silliness:

> Hail to the Headlong! the Headlong Ap-Headlong!
> All hail to the Headlong, the Headlong Ap-Headlong!
> The Headlong Ap-Headlong
> Ap-Breakneak Ap-Headlong
> Ap-Catarack Ap-Pistyll Ap-Rhaiader Ap-Headlong!

The best of these slow-paced developments in the novel is the fall of Mr. Cranium from the top of an observation tower when Milestone and Headlong set off an explosion as part of their reconstruction of the squire's park. The scene constitutes a wry echo of the first Headlong's descent from Mount Snowdon and invites understanding as an allegory of Cranium's fall from ivory-towered intelligence to the brute facts of a physical world, but the allegory is throwaway inasmuch as the fall mirrors no discernible change in Cranium's outlook. Indeed, Peacock's elaborate retard on his syntax combines with an excessive nicety of moment-to-moment description to rob the scene of all physical and psychological reality. Cranium is only a verbal entity bouncing in slow motion down a string of dilatory clauses:

> The tower remained untouched: but the Squire, in his consolatory reflections, had omitted the consideration of the influence of sudden fear, which had so violent an effect on Mr. Cranium, who was just commencing a speech concerning the very fine prospect from the top of the tower, that, cutting short the thread of his observations, he bounded, under the elastic influence of terror, several feet into the air. His ascent being unluckily a little out of the perpendicular, he descended with a proportionate curve from the apex of his projection, and alighted, not on the wall of the tower, but in an ivy-bush by its side, which, giving way beneath him, transferred him to a tuft of hazel at its base, which, after upholding him an instant, consigned him to the boughs of an ash that had rooted itself in a fissure about half way down the rock, which finally transmitted him to the waters below.

In the context of so much high-spirited camping, it may seem odd that Peacock allows his philosophers to make good points in argument, not continually, but often enough to cast a shadow of seriousness over the auctorial shenanigans and the pseudo-scholarship that the characters press upon each other. On at least one occasion when Escot is holding forth upon human deterioration, Mr. Foster is permitted a sober wisdom:

> I should be sorry that such an opinion should become universal, independently of my conviction of its fallacy. Its general admission would tend, in a great measure, to produce the very evils it appears to lament. What could be its effect, but to check the ardour of investigation, to extinguish the zeal of philanthropy, to freeze the current of enterprising hope, to bury in the torpor of skepticism and in the stagnation of despair, every better faculty of the human mind, which will necessarily become retrograde in ceasing to be progressive?

Escot is allowed an equal wisdom and considerable eloquence when he objects to Foster's vision of the industrial revolution as a source of new comforts and conveniences:

> To what end? to contract the sum of human wants? to teach the art of living on a little? to disseminate independence, liberty, and health? No; to multiply factitious desires, to stimulate depraved appetites, to invent unnatural wants, to heap up incense on the shrine of luxury, and accumulate expedients of selfish and ruinous profusion. . . . *Every new want you invent for civilized man is a new instrument of torture for him who cannot indulge it.* [emphasis mine]

Even MacLaurel is permitted a moment of affecting truth. Denounced by Escot for being in the employ of a periodical that serves the ends of individuals and of a political party, he responds with Dickensian dignity, "Ye ken, sir, a mon mun leeve."

To view Peacock only, or mainly, as a satirist runs the risk of attending inadequately to such moments of seriousness as these. Any theory of comedy in *Headlong Hall* has to come to terms with an auctorial affection for the characters that not only indulges their lunacy but permits them to be forceful and even impressive on occasion. It is not enough to say that Peacock had little impulse to reach for the definitive truth or that he was content to allow conflicting views to play off each other, striking occasional sparks of truth, for his fictional manner is too dexterous, too quietly impudent, and too distinctly camp to be rationalized so. Were Peacock a more conventional satirist, he would have dissolved his crocheteers' differences in irony or in some overarching point of view, but with the distinctive fondness of a camp humorist for his subject he preferred to leave them a small measure of dignity, unassimilated by any larger scheme of understanding.

Yet the crocheteers are not eternally at loggerheads, either. If differences of viewpoint are not resolved in *Headlong Hall,* most arguments are effectively terminated by invitations to the table or to share a bottle of wine, and most of the characters are profoundly at one in the pleasure with which they both give and receive hospitality. Indeed, the passions for talk and for conviviality are almost indistinguishable in Peacock's world, as they were in his person. To speak one's mind however closed it might be is a civilized courtesy, like passing the Madeira or filling a bumper or joining in a chorus. No person of sense will snigger.

Nightmare Abbey (1818)

Nightmare Abbey, the most esteemed of Peacock's seven novels, has a more focused subject than *Headlong Hall* in its general concern with Gothic fiction and its specific concern with the reader of such fiction. Like Jane Austen, whose *Northanger Abbey* was published in the same year as *Nightmare Abbey,* Peacock disdained the runaway fashion for Germanic gloom and melancholy that he attributed to the influence of Lord Byron and *Childe Harold's Pilgrimage.* In a letter to Shelley written when *Nightmare Abbey* was almost ready for the publisher, he confided that his intention was "to bring to a sort of philosophic focus a few of the morbidities of modern literature, and to let in a little daylight on its atrabilarious complexion."[8] "I think it necessary to 'make a stand' against the 'encroachments' of black bile," he had written earlier to Shelley. "The fourth canto of *Childe Harold* is really too bad. I cannot consent to be *auditor tantum* of this systematical 'poisoning' of the 'mind' of the 'reading public.'"[9]

Peacock's basic conceit in the novel is that melancholy has become the genius loci of the eponymous Nightmare Abbey, a mansion positioned between the sea and the fens in rural Lincolnshire. There Scythrop Glowry and his father dwell in stylized gloom, Mr. Glowry despairing eternally of both love and friendship, Scythrop recently disappointed in a love match with Miss Emily Girouette. A cadre of servants selected for long faces and macabre names intensifies the melancholy spirit of the place: a butler named

Raven, a steward named Crow, a valet named Skellet (French: *squelette,* skeleton), and grooms named Mattocks and Graves. A footman who styled himself Diggory Deathshead was once hired for the cachet of his name, but he proved intolerably mirthful:

> On Diggory's arrival, Mr. Glowry was horror-struck by the sight of a round ruddy face, and a pair of laughing eyes. Deathshead was always grinning,—not a ghastly smile, but the grin of a comic mask; and disturbed the echoes of the hall with so much unhallowed laughter, that Mr. Glowry gave him his discharge. Diggory, however, had staid long enough to make conquests of all the old gentleman's maids, and left him a flourishing colony of young Deathsheads to join chorus with the owls, that had before been the exclusive choristers of Nightmare Abbey.

The Glowry taste for solitude and melancholic musing does not preclude hospitality, and for most of the novel Mr. Glowry is host to a gathering of crocheteers, like Squire Headlong before him. Chief among his guests are the transcendental philosopher Mr. Flosky, who likes to wrap all ideas in mystery; Mr. Toobad, a "Manichaean Millenarian" fond of proclaiming "The Devil is come upon you, having great wrath"; and the fashionably languid Mr. Listless, the most likable of the three. Also present is a passionate ichthyologist, Mr. Asterias, who is in pursuit of a mermaid rumored to be haunting the Lincolnshire coast; the poet Mr. Cypress, a morbid and self-dramatizing young man who is about to leave England for Greece; and the Reverend Mr. Larynx, an obliging divine always ready to sympathize with Mr. Glowry, drink Madeira with Scythrop, quote Revelations with Mr. Toobad, or lament the lost days of feudal darkness with Mr. Flosky. The only guest present but not really welcome at Nightmare Abbey is Mr. Hilary, an inexplicably good-humored relation of the Glowries.

The plot of *Nightmare Abbey* is based on the vacillation of Scythrop Glowry between two women, the coquettish Marionetta Celestina O'Carroll, to whom he finds himself vaguely engaged, and a mysterious "Stella" who appears one day in his study seeking protection from what she terms an "atrocious persecution" by her father. With her aura of dark mystery and her fund of philosophical abstractions, Stella immediately fascinates Scythrop. An accommodating sort, he is soon affianced to her as well as to Marionetta, and when that situation becomes public "Stella" is revealed to be Mr. Toobad's daughter Celinda, who had been fleeing a marriage her father wished to arrange for her with—ironically—Scythrop himself. Unable to choose between the two women when pressed to do so and rejected by both for his indecision, Scythrop calls for "a pint of port and a pistol" with which to imitate the suicide of Goethe's Werther. Mr. Glowery persuades him to delay the fateful moment, and through his agency Scythrop hears a week later of Celinda's betrothal to Flosky and Marionetta's betrothal to Listless. In the last line of the novel the pistol is forgotten, and Scythrop commands Raven, "Bring some Madeira."

The roman à clef correspondences of *Nightmare Abbey* make a stronger claim to attention than those of *Headlong Hall* inasmuch as they configure something of an allegorical drama. Mr. Cypress suggests Lord Byron in that he speaks a continual patchwork of sentimental jargon and of actual lines from *Childe Harold's Pilgrimage,* but he is allowed the stage for only one chapter—a meaningful limitation, as it was commonplace between 1816 and 1818 to attribute the general rage for gloom and misanthropy in England to the publication of *Childe Harold.* Mr. Flosky is a second caricature of Coleridge,[10] his speeches replete with allusions to German metaphysics, to the *Biographia Literaria,* and to the *Lay Sermons,* and he is almost continually on stage in Coleridge's role as the preeminent English apologist for German romanticism. What Peacock seems to have understood very well and to have suggested by the different presence he allowed Cypress and Flosky is that the complex of ideas that constitutes English romanticism received its primary impetus in Germany and continued to be nourished there and in England by philosophic subjectivity. Byron, he suggests, was merely a popularizer; Coleridge was a more pernicious agent in the breakdown of good sense and right feeling, therefore a maker of no sense whatsoever in the world of *Nightmare Abbey.*

Yet it is not the omnipresent Flosky who holds center stage in Peacock's allegory but Scythrop Glowry, who suggests the poet Percy Bysshe Shelley in his schemes to regenerate mankind and in his taste for unbridled melodrama in both literature and life. In Scythrop's inability to choose between Marionetta and Stella, Peacock seems even to replicate the situation in which Shelley found himself during the summer of 1814, when he wanted to cohabit with both his wife, Harriet Westbrook, and his mistress, Mary Godwin. Little else suggests that the character is the man, however, and the identification of Scythrop with Shelley is considerably less forceful than the identification of Cypress with Byron and of Flosky with Coleridge. Probably it was not obvious at all to contemporary readers of the novel, for Shelley's private affairs were not matters of general knowledge in 1818.[11] Shelley himself seems to have been insensitive to the general likeness, and in a letter to Peacock he praised *Nightmare Abbey* without apparent self-consciousness. If he realized that Peacock had borrowed several aspects of his mind and situation for the character of Scythrop Glowry, he must have credited the alembic of creation:

> I am delighted with Nightmare Abbey. I think Scythrop a character admirably conceived & executed, & I know not how to praise sufficiently the lightness chastity & strength of the language of the whole. It perhaps exceeds all your works in this. I suppose the moral is contained in what Falstaff says "For God's sake talk like a man of this world" and yet looking deeper into it, is not the misdirected enthusiasm of Scythrop what J[esus] C[hrist] calls the salt of the earth?[12]

Given center stage in the allegory, Scythrop stands for Peacock's chief concern: the reader who takes black-bile literature too much to heart. It does not constitute a criticism of Shelley that Scythrop is an enthusiast who prefers ideology to good sense, however much that general failing may have been Shelley's, for Scythrop is essentially a victim without meaningful resonance in the roman à clef. He is representative for that reason of all victims of the new sensibility. Mr. Glowry, Mr. Listless, and Marionetta suffer derangements akin to his, and their common deliverance from the agents of black bile has the force of allegoric generalization. Indeed, good sense and cheerfulness are implicitly restored at the end of the novel as if the fashion for melancholia had posed no real threat to the literary scene. Cypress is packed off to Greece; Flosky, distracted by a wife as disengaged from reality as he; Scythrop, comforted with Madeira sans pistol. In this allegorical reading of the roman à clef, Scythrop is Peacock's Everyman—a naif in whom sunny good sense will always triumph over transcendental darkness.

Nightmare Abbey loses much of its comedic richness if such roman à clef correspondences and allegorical implications dominate the reader's attention, however. As in the case of *Headlong Hall,* most of the pseudophilosophical discussions among its characters are appreciable as comedy without any special insight into the cultural circumstances of their composition. When Mr. Flosky pronounces that "tea, late dinners, and the French Revolution have played the devil . . . and brought the devil into play," the scene is enriched if the reader knows that the devils in question are blue devils (or "phantoms of indigestion"); that Lady Byron's social circle styled itself *The Blues;* that, politically speaking, a *blue* usually means a Tory; and that the fashionable hour for dinner was gradually growing later in the day during Peacock's lifetime. But the comic crux of the scene is Mr. Listless bestirring himself to say, "Tea, late dinner, and the French Revolution. I cannot exactly see the connection of ideas." His temerity sends Mr. Flosky into a dither of transcendental opacity and logical subversion that is climaxed with a dazzling non sequitur. If the majestic absurdity of Flosky's response is unfair to Coleridge on the level of roman à clef, the tongue-in-cheek extravagance of his absurdity is entertainingly camp:

I should be very sorry if you could; I pity the man who can see the connection of his own ideas. Still more do I pity him, the connection of whose ideas any other person can see. Sir, the great evil is, that there is too much commonplace light in our moral and political literature; and light is a great enemy to mystery, and mystery is a great friend to enthusiasm. . . . Synthetical reasoning, setting up as its goal some unattainable abstraction, like an imaginary quantity in algebra, and commencing its course with taking for granted some two assertions which cannot be proved, from the union of these two assumed truths produces a third assumption, and so on in infinite series, to the unspeakable benefit of the human intellect. The beauty of this process is, that at every step it strikes out into two branches, in a compound ratio of ramification; so that you are perfectly sure of losing your way, and keeping your mind in perfect health, by the perpetual exercise of an interminable quest; and for these reasons I have christened my eldest son Emmanuel Kant Flosky.

A scene of equally rich comedy that needs no reference to roman à clef correspondences occurs when Scythrop suggests to Marionetta that they imitate Rosalia and Don Carlos in Grosse's *Horrid Mysteries* by opening veins in each other's arms, mixing their blood in a bowl, and drinking the mixture as a sacrament of love. No student of black bile, Marionetta turns green and flees.

Scythrop pursued her, crying, "Stop, stop, Marionetta—my life, my love!" and was gaining rapidly on her flight, when, at an ill-omened corner, where two corridors ended in an angle, at the head of a staircase, he came into sudden and violent contact with Mr. Toobad, and they both plunged together to the foot of the stairs, like two billiard-balls into one pocket. This gave the young lady time to escape, and enclose herself in her chamber; while Mr. Toobad, rising slowly, and rubbing his knees and shoulders, said, "You see, my dear Scythrop, in this little incident, one of the innumerable proofs of the temporary supremacy of the devil; for what but a systematic design and concurrent contrivance of evil could have made the angles of time and place coincide in our unfortunate persons at the head of this accursed staircase?"

The comedy of this scene has many facets, of course: the literalization of Scythrop's and Toobad's respective obsessions in the figure of the two corridors; the trivialization of their mental collision in the image of the two billiard balls; the fine counterpoint of Scythrop's impassioned cry, Marionetta's queasy stomach, and Mr. Toobad's formal eloquence. Other details create suspense in a comically formulaic way: Scythrop gaining rapidly in his flight; the corner being ill-omened; Mr. Toobad rising slowly. But the genius of the scene is Peacock's creative pleasure shining through such contrivances. His pleasure is especially manifest in the indulgent pacing of the scene, which allows each element a full and leisurely flowering in defiance of the convulsive activity in which the characters are engaged.

At its best, Peacock's comedy is built of just such indulgences of the creative moment. Plotting and satire take second place to flourishes so varied in kind as to seem camp whimsies rather than the components of a disciplined style. Witty, unexpected phrases mock clichés of the Gothic novel but impress themselves as incidental bon mots, as when Scythrop's mother is described as "an accomplished scold," his father as "a very consolate widower," and the view from Nightmare Abbey as "a fine monotony of fens and windmills." Adorning the text like furbelows are similes that strive for epigrammatic crispness but are comically labored, as when Scythrop is said after his schooling to be "like a well-threshed ear of corn, with nothing in his head" and when Nightmare Abbey is said to be "no better than a spacious kennel, for every one in it led the life of a dog." Indeed, Peacock's much-praised style is largely a camp joke. His syntax strives for formal balance less in tribute to a lost ideal of eighteenth-century prose than in spasmodic, tongue-in-cheek attempts to lend shape to the vagaries of human behavior:

He [Mr. Glowry] had been deceived in an early friendship: he had been crossed in love; and had offered his hand, from pique, to a lady, who accepted it from interest, and who, in so doing, violently tore asunder the bonds of a tried and youthful attachment.

Again,

At the house of Mr. Hilary, Scythrop first saw the beautiful Miss Emily Girouette. He fell in love; which is nothing new. He was favorably received; which is nothing strange. Mr. Glowry and Mr. Girouette had a meeting on the occasion, and quarrelled about the terms of the bargain; which is neither new nor strange. The lovers were torn asunder, weeping and vowing everlasting constancy; and, in three weeks after this tragical event, the lady was led a smiling bride to the altar, by the Honourable Mr. Lackwit; which is neither strange nor new.

A joke sustained longer than its comic energies warrant is a favorite Pavonine indulgence. Mr. Listless is so entirely lethargic that he has handed over his memory to his French valet, Fatout. When the Reverend Mr. Larynx proposes a game of billiards, Listless says, "Really I should be very happy; but, in my present exhausted state, the exertion is too much for me. I do not know when I have been equal to such an effort. Fatout! when did I play at billiards last?" Lectured by Mr. Asterias on mermaids, he says, "I have been much on the sea-shore, in the season, but I do not think I ever saw a mermaid. Fatout! did I ever see a mermaid?" On the discovery that a ghost seems to haunt Nightmare Abbey, he asks predictably, "Fatout! did I ever see a ghost?" Although a good joke to begin with, the lazy reliance of Listless on Fatout's memory is progressively funnier not for itself but for Peacock's impudence in building it to an epistemological climax without any other comic refinement and without a discernible contribution to the narrative advance.

It is the same auctorial impudence that the reader appreciates in an incidental spoof of Edmund Burke's solemnly scientific analysis of the outward signs of love. "The head reclines something on one side," opined Burke in his *Philosophical Enquiry,* "the eye-lids are more closed than usual, and the eyes roll gently with an inclination to the object; the mouth is a little opened, and the breath draws slowly, with now and then a low sigh."[13] Peacock sustains his spoof of this passage inordinately—out-Heroding

Herod, as it were—but his capricious lip-homage to Burke's method is the joke:

> Scythrop . . . threw himself into his arm-chair, crossed his left foot over his right knee, placed the hollow of his left hand on the interior ancle of his left leg, rested his right elbow on the elbow of the chair, placed the ball of his right thumb against his right temple, curved the forefinger along the upper part of his forehead, rested the point of the middle finger on the bridge of his nose, and the points of the two others on the lower part of the palm, fixed his eyes intently on the veins in the back of his left hand, and sat in this position like the immoveable Theseus. . . . We hope the admirers of the *minutiae* in poetry and romance will appreciate this accurate description of a pensive attitude.

Peacock's indulgence of his auctorial whims is nowhere more clear than in the combined admiration and fascination with which he views his crocheteers. A character like Mr. Hilary is standard in a Pavonine novel and seems intended to throw the eccentricity of the other characters into relief, but in fact he is barely utilized in that capacity. Peacock so greatly admires the crocheteers' mental vitality and is so greatly fascinated by their strangeness that he has little impulse to introduce such a reasonable person into their scenes. Effectively, Peacock finds himself charmed by creations he had meant to scorn, as Fielding—not the least of Peacock's mentors in his craft—seems to have found himself charmed by the character Joseph Andrews. Thus, when an obsessive like Mr. Asterias is permitted a gratuitous increase of certainty that he has sighted a mermaid, no reasonable voice is permitted to undermine the towering edifice of his illogic. Indeed, the parodic force of the scene is wholly eclipsed by the sweetness of Asterias's self-delusion. "Whatever else it might be, it certainly was not a fisherman," he ponders. "It might be a lady . . . it might be one of the female servants . . . it could scarcely be a stranger . . . might it not be a mermaid? It was possibly a mermaid. It was probably a mermaid. It was very probably a mermaid. Nay, what else could it be but a mermaid? It certainly was a mermaid."

Peacock is harsher with Flosky than with Asterias, of course, but even that transcendental philosopher is allowed a syllogistic capriccio, the madness of which is more charming than disturbing:

> He had been in his youth an enthusiast for liberty, and had hailed the dawn of the French Revolution as the promise of a day that was to banish

war and slavery, and every form of vice and misery, from the face of the earth. Because all this was not done, he deduced that nothing was done; and from this deduction, according to his system of logic, he drew a conclusion that worse than nothing was done; that the overthrow of the feudal fortresses of tyranny and superstition was the greatest calamity that had ever befallen mankind.

The success of such camp humor in *Nightmare Abbey* makes clear the pivotal role played in the genre by an author's attitude toward eccentric characters. Crocheteers cease to be objects of satire when they are admired for the vitality with which they become their hobbyhorses, are allowed their heads in an auctorial fascination with their strangeness, and are set loose in a mad steeplechase of the mind. Indeed, they become occasions of a mode of comedy in which the laughter that might constitute social correction delights instead in all that is innocently odd. How unfortunate that, after Peacock, the camp mode of humor disappeared from English fiction for almost one hundred years.[14] Peacock would have had to look far into the future, past Mrs. Elizabeth Gaskell, Thackeray, Dickens, Trollope, the Brontës, George Eliot, Samuel Butler, and George Meredith, to find in the Edwardian age an aesthetic of the novel once again sympathetic to camping, and to find in novelists like Beerbohm and Firbank the heirs of his especial insouciance.

3

The Triumph of Fantasy: Max Beerbohm

Although it is among the most sweet-tempered and beloved of books, Max Beerbohm's *Zuleika Dobson; or, An Oxford Love Story* tends to pit its devotees against its critics. Central to their disagreements is a question about the sort of novel that *Zuleika Dobson* is—a fantasy, a satire, a fantasy edged with satire, or something else altogether. In a rebuke of critics who consider it a satire, E. M. Forster proclaimed it in 1927 "the most consistent achievement of *fantasy* in our time" [emphasis mine],[1] and Beerbohm effectively endorsed Forster's view in a note he appended in 1946 to the first Modern Library edition of the novel:

> When, in 1911, this book was first published, some people seemed to think it was intended as a satire on such things as the herd instinct, as feminine coquetry, as snobbishness, even as legerdemain; whereas I myself had supposed it was just a fantasy; and as such, I think, it should be regarded by others.[2]

Critics immediately took issue with Beerbohm's endorsement of Forster's view. The legacy of Peacock's camp counting for nothing, Louis Kronenberger diagnosed "a slight crudeness about *Zuleika* and a slight unpalatability"; Beerbohm, he said, had not quite managed "to dissolve the real in the fantastic."[3] Agreeing with Kronenberger, Edmund Wilson suggested that the fantastic and the real, instead of being interwoven neatly, had gotten themselves into a kind of snarl. "What is the pattern or the point of *Zuleika?*" he asked querulously. "Is it a satire or parody or nonsense or what?"[4] Beerbohm liked to keep audiences uncertain about his distinctive mix of irony and whimsy, one suspects—apparently so from his earliest years. It is said that when traveling by train to Croydon as a youth he was asked why he had suddenly lowered the blinds. "S-sh!" he answered. "Lest I should see the Crystal

Palace."[5] In such fanciful hyperbole it is almost impossible to disentangle the ingenuous and the disingenuous. The mix was the same many years later when he remarked famously in conversation, "They were a tense and peculiar family, the Oedipuses, weren't they?"[6]

In comparing the unfinished draft of *Zuleika Dobson* that Beerbohm wrote in London in 1899 and the draft he completed in Rapallo in 1911, the playwright S. N. Behrman discovered that Beerbohm himself had apparently no clear concept of what *Zuleika Dobson* was to become when he embarked upon its writing. The earlier manuscript Behrman describes as "scraggly, written in random columns and riddled with doodles—of Balfour, Disraeli, Reginald Turner, Henry James, Oscar Wilde, Henry Irving, Lord Ribbesdale, Edward VII." "Often the graphic seems to gain the upper hand," he notes; "several times, Max seems to have forgotten that he was writing a novel, and whole pages are devoted to drawings, some of them sketches for caricatures that later became famous."[7] The Rapallo manuscript, on the other hand, contains no doodles but many erasures, as if Beerbohm were concerned to excise all elements of caricature.

Whatever the exact mix of irony and whimsy in Beerbohm's masterpiece, it is one of the fundamental texts of camp. In *The Happy Hypocrite* and especially in his drawings Beerbohm further indulged his instinct for camp humor, but nowhere with more effervescence than in *Zuleika Dobson.*

Zuleika Dobson (1911)

The catastrophic event of *Zuleika Dobson* is set in motion immediately when the title character descends upon fin de siècle Oxford to visit her grandfather, the warden of Judas College.[8] Zuleika Dobson is not classically beautiful—the narrator suggests that "a Greek would have railed at her asymmetry, and an Elizabethan have called her 'gipsy'"—but she has parlayed her physical charms into an international career as a conjurer. Indeed, she is an archetypal femme fatale in the tradition of Shakespeare's Cleopatra, and the Oxford undergraduates fall in love with her en masse. Most notable among her conquests is the fourteenth "Duke of Dorset, Marquis of Dorset, Earl of Grove, Earl of Chastermaine, Viscount Brewsby, Baron Grove, Baron Petstrap, and Baron Wolock." His aristocratic hauteur attracts Zuleika profoundly because she longs for a man to look up to and adore, but as soon as the duke grovels before her with the other infatuates she scorns his offer of marriage. The duke then decides to die for love—a decision he soon regrets but cannot honorably reverse. Dressed in his elaborate robes as a Knight of the Garter, he commits suicide by throwing himself into the Isis during the annual boat race among the Oxford colleges. With the exception of a coward named Noaks the entire undergraduate population follows his lead, all for love of Zuleika, and even Noaks throws himself to his death a few days later. When Zuleika explains the magnitude of the disaster to her grandfather, the warden of Judas suggests that she might, perhaps, leave Oxford and not visit it again in term-time. Nothing is left for her except to board a special train for Cambridge.[9]

Even in so brief a summary of the plot, one can appreciate that conventional hyperbole tends to become literal fact in *Zuleika Dobson*. The heroine is a femme fatale actually fatal to hundreds of men in a single afternoon; she really does intend to surrender all for love; and dons who have joked too casually about preferring an Oxford empty of students find their quadrangles abruptly depopulated. The notion that death is preferable to life without love is not a romantic whimsy in *Zuleika Dobson* but a conviction upon which hundreds of persons truly act, and it is obviously no joke to speak of the New Woman's presence in Oxford as a violation of male sanctuary. When two black owls perch on the battlements of the duke's ancestral home, they are not the spirit of gothicism run amok but a sober prognostication, and the duke immediately orders the family vault prepared for his funeral. The spirit of Chopin comes literally to life for the duke's rendition of the *Marche Funèbre,* and George Sand attends Chopin's resuscitation in a ghostly literalization of the commonplace that love is stronger than death. Busts of Roman emperors look down upon Oxford from pedestals that intersperse a railing around the Sheldonian Theatre and watch the developing events with real, not figurative consciousness:

They, at least, foresaw the peril that was overhanging Oxford, and they gave such warning as they could. Let that be remembered to their credit. Let that incline us to think more gently of them. In their lives we know, they were infamous, some of them—"nihil non commiserunt stupri, saevitiae, impietatis." But are they too little punished, after all? Here in Oxford, exposed eternally and inexorably to heat and frost, to the four winds that lash them and the rains that wear them away, they are expiating, in effigy, the abominations of their pride and cruelty and lust. Who were lechers, they are without bodies; who were tyrants, they are crowned never but with crowns of snow; who made themselves even with the gods, they are by American visitors frequently mistaken for the Twelve Apostles.

Beerbohm winks at the reader in making such conceits the reality of his fictional world, of course, and he is at pains to ground his conceits in the stuff of everyday experience. Even his story of so many lives lost in a romantic gesture has basis in a familiar history if Matthew Arnold was right in describing Oxford as the "home of lost causes . . . and impossible loyalties."[10] Certainly Beerbohm's Oxford is the authentic place, the busts of Roman emperors on the Sheldonian railing as familiar a part of the mise-en-scène as the mists from Christ Church meadow, and encounters that he describes on the Broad as much a cipher of the life of Oxford as the babel of its clocks and spires. Oxford's sense of its privileged existence and pride in its history are captured exactly—nowhere better than in the anecdote of poor Pedby, the Junior Fellow upon whom falls the duty of reading a Latin grace after the mass suicide of the students. The false quantities of the young mathematician's Latin are at first a scandal to the assembled dons, then, in Oxford's eternal alembic, a treasure for the ages:

Suddenly, unheralded, a thing of highest destiny had fallen into their academic midst. The stock of Common Room talk had to-night been reinforced and enriched for all time. Summers and winters would come and go, old faces would vanish, giving place to new, but the story of Pedby's grace would be told always. Here was a tradition that generations of dons yet unborn would cherish and chuckle over. Something akin to awe mingled itself with the subsiding merriment.

Insouciantly, Beerbohm allows his readers continual awareness that his fairy-tale fantasy is under siege by a cruder, more venal, physically importunate world. On the one hand, Zuleika's pearl earrings and the duke's pearl studs change colors in a barometric response to fluctuations in the couple's relationship; on the other hand, when dressed in the mulberry-colored and brass-buttoned coat that is the uniform of his exclusive dining club, the duke is easily mistaken for a footman. "It does not do to think of such things," shudders the narrator in mock horror. Financial calculations tarnish the most dramatic moments. When the duke takes leave of his landlady to commit suicide, he is scrupulously careful not to overpay his account, and scores of women who see him gorgeously attired just moments before his suicide spend the time less in admiration of his figure than in calculating the cost of his velvet mantle at four guineas a yard. Regretting at an earlier point that he has pledged himself to suicide, the duke reflects melodramatically that "of all deaths, the bitterest that can befall a man is that he lay down his life to flatter the woman he deems vilest of her sex"—then he sneezes, having caught a cold when Zuleika doused him with her water jug. In a triumph of the quotidian over stylized posture, the duke's self-importance evaporates with his dignity:

> What care now, what use, for deportment? He walked coweringly round and round his room, with frantic gestures, with head bowed. He shuffled and slunk. His dressing-gown had the look of a gabardine.

Even the carefully staged moment of the duke's suicide is flogged, for the duke has to throw himself into the water precipitously when it starts to rain upon the elaborate robes in which he has decked himself. "His very mantle was aspersed," cries a shocked narrator. "In another minute he would stand sodden, inglorious, a mock."

The play of a high style against a higher awareness of that style's absurdity is especially characteristic of *Zuleika Dobson*. In effect, Beerbohm's tendency to ape the mandarin style of Henry James (a style he greatly admired) is self-mocked by a drift toward the purple patch. The description of Zuleika's arrival in Oxford establishes that drift immediately:

> Came a whistle from the distance. The breast of an engine was descried, and a long train curving after it, under a flight of smoke. It grew and grew. Louder and louder, its noise foreran it. It became a furious, enormous monster, and, with an instinct for safety, all men receded from the platform's margin. (Yet came there with it, unknown to them, a danger far more terrible than itself.) Into the station it came blustering, with cloud and clangour. Ere it had yet stopped, the door of one carriage flew open, and from it, in a white travelling-dress, in a toque a-twinkle with fine diamonds, a lithe and radiant creature slipped nimbly down to the platform.

Louder and louder, its noise foreran it. One's pleasure in such a sentence is based partially on its fin de siècle decadence: the syntactical inversion, the vaguely archaistic but very elegant *fore-ran,* the mellifluous, somewhat heavy-footed symmetries of *louder . . . louder* and *its . . . it.* That such ornamentation is hypertrophied constitutes a parody of aesthetic fine writing, to be sure, but its hypertrophia constitutes at the same time an affectionate tribute to the fin de siècle style, for no sensitive reader can fail to recognize the delight with which Beerbohm makes the style his own. Similarly dense effects are wrought by the inversions of *came a whistle from the distance* and *into the station it came blustering;* by the archaistic elegance of *descried, receded,* and *ere it had yet stopped;* and by the exaggerated symmetries of *cloud and clangour* and *a toque a-twinkle.* Any number of sentences that manifest the same balance of fine writing, parody, and stylistic tribute might be plucked from the text. Of Zuleika's cheval glass the narrator says, "It was framed in ivory, and of fluted ivory were the slim columns it swung between." Of the duke he says, "The dandy must be celibate, cloistral; is, indeed, but a monk with a mirror for beads and breviary—an anchorite mortifying his soul that his body may be perfect." Of sympathetic neighbors who gather around the duke's landlady after his suicide, he says they are "women of her own age and kind, capacious of tragedy; women who might be relied on; founts of ejaculation, wells of surmise, downpours of remembered premonitions."

The overwrought character of such passages tends to gloss passages less clearly touched with parody—that passage, for instance, in which the monody of Great Tom, a bell that for centuries has tolled the Oxford curfew, becomes a threnody for a generation of students that will never answer to the curfew again. The stately cadence of the narrator's sentences, phrase chiming after phrase, results in an aesthetical set piece rendered wonderfully droll in the context of too much fine writing:

> Stroke by measured and leisured stroke, the old euphonious clangour pervaded Oxford, spreading out over the meadows, along the river, audible in Iffley. But to the dim groups gathering and dispersing on either bank, and to the silent workers in the boats, the bell's message came softened, equivocal; came as a requiem for these dead.

Given so much interplay between high style and a higher awareness of that style's absurdity, should the reader take seriously Beerbohm's caution that *Zuleika Dobson* is "just a fantasy" and that no satirical or parodic comment was intended? The novel has resonance in the real world if only because fantasy must have something to fantasticate. As F. W. Dupee points out, classic fantasies like *Gulliver's Travels,* the *Alice* books, and Kafka's *Metamorphosis* take as their subject almost the whole of reality and "fantasticate the realities so thoroughly that, presto!, they come to look fantastic themselves."[11] The subject of Beerbohm's fantasy is his own dandyism, his preference for style over all else in the telling of his story—a subject more modest but no less "real" than theirs. What distinguishes his mode of fantasy from that of Swift, Dodgson, or Kafka is that the reality he fantasticates preexists in a recognizably fantastical mode. In evidence one has only to recall the aesthetic dandyism of the 1890s, of which Beerbohm was eminently a child, or the excessively slim volume of his writings that Beerbohm published cheekily at the age of twenty-four and entitled *The Works of Max Beerbohm.*[12] Because they assume rather than expose the fantastical as a component of reality, both phenomena make it impossible to understand *Zuleika Dobson* as a satiric exposé of the fantastical underpinnings of reality. Satire and camp recognize the same human foibles, of course, but satire seeks to diminish its human subjects, while camp applauds the human patchedness. *Zuleika Dobson* is clearly on that basis a work of camp inspiration, not satiric purpose.

Beerbohm's camping is particularly spirited in a series of passages in which he addresses the reader directly. He starts off in an eighteenth-century mode, addressing a "sensitive reader" and instructing him or her to "start not" at the fact that the dullard Noaks lives in the same boarding house as the duke. He goes on to assume easy camaraderie with his reader. Of a sinner having a better chance than a saint for earthly immortality, he says, "*We* in whom original sin preponderates, find him easier to understand" [emphasis mine]. But soon this genially familiar narrator affects more imaginative modes of presence. Teasing Beerbohm's relation to him, he permits Zuleika to be questioned about the literary tone to her conversation. "Ah," she responds, "that is an unfortunate trick which I caught from a writer, a Mr. Beerbohm, who once sat next to me at dinner somewhere." Shortly afterward, he makes a preposterous, speciously straightforward claim that he is writing not fantasy but history—that he has a special exemption from Clio, the muse of historians, to adopt the freedoms of a novelist. Things are decidedly out of hand when readers find themselves charged with disbelief when they had thought they were enjoying a conceit and charged with insider's knowledge that *Zuleika Dobson* is a roman à clef when it had seemed to them thoroughly fantastical. Is the narrator quite sane? His overly tactful assumption of shared knowledge is abruptly monitory, even threatening:

> I said that I was Clio's servant. And I felt, when I said it, that you looked at me dubiously, and murmured among yourselves.
>
> Not that you doubted I was somewhat connected with Clio's household. The lady after whom I have named this book is alive, and well known to some of you personally, to all of you by repute.[13] Nor had you finished my first page before you guessed my theme to be that episode in her life which caused so great a sensation among the newspaper-reading public a few years ago. (It all seems but yesterday, does it not? They are still vivid to us, those headlines. We have hardly yet ceased to be edified by the morals pointed in those leading articles.) And yet very soon you found me behaving just like any novelist—reporting the exact words that passed between the protagonists at private interviews—aye, and the exact thoughts and emotions that were in their breasts. Little wonder that you wondered! Let me make things clear to you.
>
> *I have my mistress's leave to do this.* [emphasis mine]

In the continuing reinvention of his narrative posture, the narrator goes on to become unreasonably stern with his readers. At one point he announces that they have two questions about events, then rebukes them for the questions that are really his own. "In a way, you have a perfect right to ask both these questions," he snaps with mock impatience. "But their very pertinence shows that you think I might omit things that matter. Please don't interrupt me again." When Zuleika considers becoming a nun in order to forestall hordes of Europeans from following the example of Oxford men, the narrator is stern with his readers again: "I hope you will now, despite your rather evident animus against her [Zuleika], set this to her credit: that she did, so soon as she realized the hopelessness of her case, make just that decision." In point of fact he is misleading the reader, for Zuleika recants her decision to take the veil. Yet the narrator affects to be the most scrupulous of historians. Probing the reader's opinion of Zuleika (an opinion he postulates as the reader's), he says, "She deserved to suffer, you say? Maybe. I merely state that she did suffer." As a historian he admits that he is sorely tempted to "fob off on his readers just one bright fable for effect." "Why not?" whispers Apollo seductively; "Your readers would be excited, gratified." Priggishly he answers that the eyes of Clio are upon him. He spurns his duty to Clio, however, when he insists upon giving the duke an hour of decent privacy after Zuleika empties a water jug (presumably a euphemism for her chamber pot) on his head. For that dereliction of duty he cannot and will not apologize, although Clio has abused him for it "in language less befitting a Muse than a fish-wife."

To be rebuked for interruptions they have not made and for an "evident animus" they have not felt by a narrator who prides himself on a scrupulous devotion to the facts despite an actively editing conscience, a prudish sensibility, and a privileged freedom to behave as a novelist is for most readers a giddy experience. It inspires a sense that they are only a shadow audience, eclipsed by an imagined audience more interesting and more real to the narrator than they. Moreover, that imaginary audience is only one of several that the narrator interposes between the events in Oxford and his readers. The Roman emperors on the railing of the Sheldonian and the gods in heaven attend to the events in Oxford, too, the first as if they were a Greek chorus, the second as if they were the collective genius behind Beerbohm's plot. The evocation of these several audiences has the effect of stripping from the narrator all his pretensions to being a historian and clarifying what he quintessentially is: a performer for whom the vaunt of high style is a compulsion; a performer, indeed, for whom a silent audience does not suffice; a thoroughgoing camp.

The Roman emperors are an artful foil for the narrator's histrionic compulsion as well as its product. As they stare down on Zuleika's entry into Oxford, the emperors foresee the tragedy that will unfold, and great beads of perspiration glisten on their brows. The narrator is rhapsodic: "Surely, it is a sign of some grace in them that they rejoiced not, this bright afternoon, in the evil that was to befall the city of their penance." The duke's infatuation with Zuleika is immediately clear to the emperors, their own fall from grace and power allowing them compassion, and the narrator measures the magnitude of the coming disaster by the standard of their present ignominy. It is his notion that they are a Roman chorus in a Greek tragedy transpiring in British Oxford, unable to comment vocally on the action except through his imagination but suffering terribly the pain of their foreknowledge:

> The high grim busts of the Emperors stared down at him [the duke], their faces more than ever tragically cavernous and distorted. They saw and read in that moonlight the symbols on his breast. As he stood on his doorstep, waiting for the door to be opened, he must have seemed to them a thing for infinite compassion. For were they not privy to the doom that the morrow, or the morrow's morrow, held for him—held not indeed for him alone, yet for him especially, as it were, and for him most lamentably?

It is the narrator's joke, however, that the emperors are also sentimentalists, a result, presumably, of their having spent too many centuries in English exile. A daughter of the duke's landlady has grown from a toddler to an attractive young lady as they have looked fondly on, and they cherish the hope of a romantic union between her and "a certain young gentleman," as they coyly refer to the duke. Indeed, the style in which the narrator imagines the emperors' interest in the landlady's daughter is avuncular, a send-up of the emperors' tragicalness. "The Emperors had always predicted that she would be pretty," the reader is instructed. "And very pretty she was. . . . Where in all England was a prettier, sweeter girl than their Katie?"

Completely untouched by tragedy and sentiment in their turn, the gods are a wickedly playful audience, as when they decree that a piece of orange peel should be discarded at the corner of Turl Street for the master of Balliol to slip upon. Convinced that they have sent Zuleika to destroy him, the duke decides to rebuff the gods by masterminding his own death—at which point the gods lean over the thunderclouds and roar with laughter, for they have already uncaged the owls that make his suicide inevitable. "There was nothing to demean him in that," the narrator pompously assures his readers, mock-anxious to preserve literary decorum and to dissociate his own omniscience from the gods' omnipotence. "The peripety was according to the best rules of tragic art," he insists. Against that insistence stands the narrator's disingenuousness as he explains how the gods have orchestrated the events for which he bears auctorial responsibility. Their ineptitude is an unmistakable echo of his own inability to preside with consistent voice over his narrative, their absentmindedness the equivalent of his stylistic impulsiveness; their devotion to the "felicitous touch" identical with his own:

> You must not imagine that they think out and appoint everything that is to befall us, down to the smallest detail. Generally, they just draw a sort of broad outline. . . . Thus, in the matters of which this book is record, it was they who made the Warden invite his grand-daughter to Oxford . . . and it was they who prompted the Duke to die for her on the following (Tuesday) afternoon. . . . But an oversight upset this plan. They had forgotten on Monday night to uncage the two black owls; and so it was necessary that the Duke's death should be postponed. They accordingly prompted Zuleika to save him. For the rest, they let the tragedy run its own course—merely putting in a felicitous touch here and there, or vetoing a superfluity. . . . It was no part of their scheme that the Duke, . . . instead of the Master of Balliol, came to grief over the orange peel.

In such a rococo involution of fantasy with the narrator's disingenuousness, and in such an elegant exposition of the absurd, *Zuleika Dobson* is a small masterpiece—the only kind that Beerbohm would have wanted to create. Has anyone ever been more successful than he in deprecating the outsize and the inflated without a concomitant giganticism of purpose? Effectively, *Zuleika Dobson* lightens the effect of Peacock's mode of camping by disdaining the clockwork confusions of farce, the point-for-point correspondences of satire, and the weight of serious ideas. The mature style of Henry James and the full panoply of Oxford tradition it makes lesser things than they are without in any sense mocking them; so, too, things that World War I was shortly to make inadmissible as subjects of light comedy: the death of a generation of young men, the aching loveliness of an empty Oxford, the *Liebestod* itself. So self-assured is the success of *Zuleika Dobson* that one might almost imagine Beerbohm looking ahead a decade and, in a nepotistic impulse, bequeathing the attention of his readers to Ronald Firbank. Firbank is not Beerbohm's heir in any obvious sense, but his novels owe a debt to Beerbohm's demonstration that camp could be liberated from its entangling alliances with farce, satire, and ideology.

4

Aestheticism Empurpled: Ronald Firbank

The novels of Ronald Firbank place themselves at the center of the camp tradition, if only for the fact that it has been their fate for sixty years to be thought ephemeral. Firbank himself was neurasthenic, given to nervous squirming and to cramming his rooms with flowers, and in the ongoing fallout from the Oscar Wilde scandal, his person has been compounded with the negligible plots, lacunary dialogue, and coyly fastidious characters of his fiction to create the impression of a talent too precious for conventional criticism. "Caviar for the heterosexual" his books are standardly called. "It is quite useless to write about Firbank," Cyril Connolly once warned, "—nobody who doesn't like him is going to like him."[1] E. M. Forster even viewed Firbank as a fragile butterfly, not to be broken on the rack of criticism:

> The victim is apt to reappear each time the wheel revolves, still alive, and with a reproachful expression upon its squashed face to address its tormentors in some such words as the following: "Critic! What do you? Neither my pleasure nor your knowledge has been increased. I was flying or crawling, and that is all there was to be learned about me . . . I only exist in my surroundings, and become meaningless as soon as you stretch me upon this rack."[2]

The lepidopterous viewpoint has been overdone, however. It is a scandal of modern biography that the prancing homosexual of countless anecdotes has not adequately been integrated with the Ronald Firbank who supervised his financial investments with care, and it is a scandal of letters that Firbank's densely wrought fictions are not generally recognized as milestones in the effort of the twentieth-century novel to free itself from nineteenth-century realism.[3] Certainly Firbank's novels have not proven ephemeral in their hereditaments. Evelyn Waugh pointed out the influence of Firbank on his early novels *Decline and Fall* and *Vile Bodies* and diagnosed a similar influence upon Osbert Sitwell, Carl Van Vechten, Harold Acton, William Gerhardie, and even Ernest Hemingway.[4] Ivy Compton-Burnett is generally thought to have learned her dialogic technique from Firbank, and Brigid Brophy testifies to Firbank's seminal influence upon her novel *The Finishing Touch.*[5] The influence of Firbank upon James McCourt's effervescent novel *Mawrdew Czgowchwz* is unmistakable. Laudably, some recent scholarship tends to view Firbank as a modernist.

Firbank's tentatively acknowledged place among the modernists must not obscure his place among the camps, however, for more than that of any other novelist in the English tradition his name evokes the camp enterprise. "Firbank is perhaps the inventor, certainly the fixer, of modern camp," observes Brophy. "Popes, cardinals, choirboys, nuns, flagellants, queens (both senses): all the classic camp dramatis personae are his."[6] Even more central to camp is Firbank's narrative mode—hagiographical, aesthetical, and irrepressibly amoral. Three late novels show Firbank at the height of his powers: *The Flower Beneath the Foot, Prancing Nigger,* and *Concerning the Eccentricities of Cardinal Pirelli.* They form an interesting trilogy as well, for *The Flower Beneath the Foot* is a camp vision of paradise, *Prancing Nigger* a vision of paradise on the verge of ruin, and *The Eccentricities of Cardinal Pirelli* a vision of paradise lost.

The Flower Beneath the Foot (1923)

The hagiographical genre of *The Flower Beneath the Foot* is proclaimed in its subtitle, *Being a Record of the Early Life of St. Laura de Nazianzi and the Times in Which She Lived.* The saint's story transpires not so much in a time, however, as in a place—the imaginary land of Pisuerga, which is an improbable mix of Italy, the South of France, London, and Arabia.[7] As the niece of Her Gaudiness the Duchess of Cavaljos, Laura has recently made her debut at court and has fallen in love with His Weariness Prince Yousef, who is first heir to the throne of Pisuerga. The prince credits Laura with saving him from cliché (a very Firbankian valuation), but he only pretends to love her. To Her Dreaminess the Queen and most of the court, Laura is "très gutter." The queen has perhaps overheard Laura at her prayers:

Oh! help me heaven to be decorative and to do right! Let me always look young, never more than sixteen or seventeen—at the *very* outside, and let Yousef love me—as much as I do him. And I thank you for creating such a darling, God (for he's a perfect dear), and I can't tell you how much I love him; especially when he wags it! I mean his tongue. . . .

Upon discovering that the prince is newly affianced to the English Princess Elsie and has had a number of mistresses—one of them black—Laura decides to enter the Convent of the Flaming-Hood:

"I thank Thee God for this *escape,*" she murmured, falling to her knees before the silver branches of a cross. "It is terrible; for I did so love him. . . . .
. . . .
. . . .
. . . .
. . . . and oh how could he ever, with a *negress?* . . . .
. . . .
. . . .
. . . .
Pho. . . . .
. . . . I fear this complete upset has considerably aged me. . . . .
. . . . but to Thee I cling". . . .

It is presumably as a nun that Laura proceeds to win sainthood, but only the subtitle, two epigraphs, and a single footnote allude to her future blessedness. Indeed, in the confessional tradition of Saint Augustine, Firbank's tale of Saint Laura de Nazianzi sketches a varied erotic life. Turning from her delight in how the prince "wags it," Laura joins a lesbianic sisterhood given to erotic flagellation, and though she has no apparent taste for the lash, she is greatly drawn to Sister Ursula, whose kisses she prefers to the prince's. Intermittently, Laura is also a narcissistic Salome, who pirouettes "interestingly" before her mirror in the last stages of dishabille and does "a thousand (and one) things besides." *Always a humiliating recollection with her in after years,* insists a fervid footnote. In the reader's last glimpse of the future saint, Laura is recoiling from an invitation to birch Sister Ursula but beating her own hands on the broken glass embedded in the convent walls and moaning, "Yousef, Yousef, Yousef. . . ." The ellipsis is everything—a symptom of unfocused, omnisexual yearning. It is as suggestive as the ellipses in Laura's prayers and as portentous as the yawning ellipses in her story.

In those narrative ellipses, Firbank amasses details of life in the world of Pisuerga and makes that imaginary land the real subject of his fiction. Pisuerga is a sort of lotusland, in which waltzes are invariably "drowsy, intricate, caressing," in which rooms are "carved-ceiled and rather lofty," and in which telephones are "wrought in ormolu and rock-crystal." Indeed, all is lushly outré in Pisuerga. Jardinieres overflow with flowering plants everywhere, and canopied recesses in the palace have been artfully denuded of their statues "in order that they might appear suggestive." Omnipresent pages giggle suggestively in corners; ladies of the court coax ecclesiastics from acolytes "in order that they might officiate at Masses, Confessions and Breakfast-parties"; and a noted "*screen artiste*" creates a sensation in the promenade by riding an Arabian mare with powdered withers and eyes made up with kohl.[8]

Both the permanent and the temporary residents of Pisuerga have names and titles archly absurd, like "His Naughtyness," "Her Dreaminess," "Lord Limpless," "Countess Medusa," "Queen Thleeanouhee."[9] The vacuous British ambassador is "Sir Somebody Something"; the proprietress of a brothel is the aggressively chic "Madame Wetme"; and a pair of clergymen are afflicted with the titles "Father Picpus" and "Father Nostradamus." The dispositional tendencies of such characters are as preposterous as their names. The Countess Medusa is celebrated in court circles for her ability to assume a "tortured-animal" look. Laura receives from a pious marchioness a social announcement that she "will be birched tomorrow, and *not* today." The aged Archduchess Elizabeth of Pisuerga has the hobby of "designing, for the use of the public, sanitary, but artistic, places of necessity on a novel system of ventilation." Dignity does not wait upon such characters, even if sainthood comes inexplicably to Sister Laura. The best of them, the Archduchess Elizabeth, expires while the queen sits by her bedside writing telegrams that announce the melancholy news, POOR LIZZIE HAS CEASED ARTICULATING.

An amoral, painterly awareness tends to overwhelm all other modes of awareness in the narrative and to render the world of Pisuerga in preposterously aesthetical terms. Pseudoaestheticism is not consciously tolerated, although it is omnipresent. When Her Dreaminess proclaims that she sees life that day "in the colour of mould," the unfashionable palette of her seeing is burlesqued by His Weariness, who thereupon "protrude[s] a shade the purple violet of his tongue." Typically, the conjunction of *shade* and the finely discriminated *purple violet* aestheticizes the prince's childishly rude action to the point of making it seem innocent of malice—a matter, almost, of putting right an instance of aesthetic offense. Her Dreaminess is earlier described as "of that *magnolia* order of colouring," and the narrator's gratuitously restrictive *that* and preciously italicized *magnolia* convey nicely his passion for colors. An almost equal passion for composition is suggested when the narrator notes of Laura that "on either side of her delicate nose a large grey eye surveyed the world." So totally aesthetical is the narrator's frame of reference that he seems to perceive the future saint as if she were potentially a cubist painting, wherein her features might have composed themselves so eccentrically that the eyes' placement, one on each side of her nose, is worth remarking.

It must be emphasized that the narrator's interest in color and compositional effects is as mischievous as it is aesthetical, throwing off an inapposite suggestion of Milton here, of luridly cannibalistic blood lust there, of mauve-tinted decadence everywhere. An attaché in attendance at the reception for the king and queen of Dateland is "all white and penseroso"—no matter the ungrammatical Italian, which only underscores the extraneous allusion. At the same reception, Queen Thleeanouhee (who eats customarily off of shells) is "lost in admiration of the Royal dinner-service of scarlet plates, that looked like pools of blood upon the cloth." Is it the use of plates that she pseudoaesthetically admires? Their barbarously unchic color? Or the evocation of fresh pools of blood? The narrator's interest in bodies and their adornment is equally mischievous. Memorably, he reports that the queen's lectress has said of the prince, "One could niche an idol in his dear, dinted chin," and the countess of Tolga's toilette inspires him to a chromatic ecstasy that an orgy of alliteration renders absurd:

> the Countess had arrayed herself in a winter gown of kingfisher-tinted silk turning to turquoise, and stencilled in purple at the arms and neck with a crisp Greek-key design; while a voluminous violet veil, depending behind her to a point, half concealed a tricorne turquoise toque from which arose a shaded lilac aigrette branching several ways.

The narrator's aesthetical mischievousness tends to quash his satiric instinct. Not even British royalty can be thought seriously mocked in the novel, for in the never-never land of Pisuerga there are no matters of state, only pitfalls of language and errors of taste that invite a royal misstep. It is a wonderfully camp moment and nothing more when the king, accompanied by a shapely page of sixteen, employs the royal pronoun with what he thinks to be misdirection and says, "We'd give perfect worlds to go, by Ourselves, to bed." An exchange between the king and his physician is equally camp in the king's effort to avoid unseemly use of the word *naked:*

> "You certainly are somewhat pale, sir."
> "Whenever I go out," the King complained, "I get an impression of raised hats."
> It was seldom King William of Pisuerga spoke in the singular tense, and Doctor Babcock looked perturbed.
> "Raised hats, sir?" he murmured in impressive tones.
> "Nude heads, doctor."

One might argue, of course, that such passages are inescapably satiric—that if men and women were not foolishly reticent about sexual matters, the exchanges would not be amusing. But "satiric" implies a corrective purpose, and who would wish the Pisuergans corrected?[10] King William's habit of tucking a few long hairs back into his nose and his queen's habit of referring to Johnnie Walker whiskey as "Johnnie" belong to the realm of silliness, not satire, whatever the disputed territory between satire and silliness. Indeed, Pisuerga is so entirely a cultural outland that its follies ask to be understood as brilliantly inventive; its assaults on the queen's English, as jeux d'esprit. The corrective spirit has surely no place in the reader's delight that the favorite play of Pisuergans is Shakespeare's *Julia Sees Her,* that the heir to the throne is said to become "Arabian-Nighty" after dinner, and that the turquoise-tiled cathedral is known as *The Blue Jesus*—on the pattern of nomenclature, one supposes, of American jazz clubs. Nor can one understand that the fatuity of British nicknames is being mocked in the following conversation between the countess of Tolga and the duchess of Varna, for that fatuity is subsumed into an absurd fretwork of alarms, melting tendresse, and discreetly hinted consolations of the flesh. The camp context carries everything with it:

"I've asked Grim-lips and Ladybird, Hairy and Fluffy, Hardylegs and Bluewings, Spindleshanks and Our Lady of Furs."

"Not Nanny-goat?"

"Luckily . . ." the Countess replied, raising to her nose the heliotropes in her hand.

"Is he no better?"

"You little know, dear, what it is to be all alone with him chez soi when he thinks and sneers into the woodwork."

"Into the woodwork?"

"He addresses the ceiling, the walls, the floor—me never!"

"Dear dove."

"All I can I'm plastic."

"Can one be plastic ever enough, dear?"

"Often, but for Olga . . ." the Countess murmured, considering a little rosy ladybird on her arm.

Arch and implicational, but satirically and morally weightless, such scenes give the world of Pisuerga its light-as-air density. Was ever a love scene written with a lighter touch than that which transpires finally between the duchess and her Olga as they drift aimlessly in a green-lanterned barge caught in the scarlet radiance of sunset's afterglow? Was ever the art of ellipsis practiced more winsomely to an aesthetical end?

"Oh, Olga!"

"Oh, Vi!"

". . . I hope you've enough money for the boat, dear? . . . ?"

". . . !!?"

"Tell me, Olga: Is my hat all sideways?"

". . . . ."

Prancing Nigger (1924)

Prancing Nigger—originally entitled "Sorrow in Sunlight"[11]—is quintessentially a novel of the tropical islands. Conceived in Havana, begun in the British West Indies, completed in Bordighera, and set on an imaginary Caribbean island named Tacarigua, it takes its spirit from Gauguin's Tahiti and from Somerset Maugham's fictionalization of Gauguin's experience in *The Moon and Sixpence.* Like most such novels, it might as well be set in the Garden of Eden, for Mrs. Ahmadou Mouth and her husband, whom she calls "Prancing Nigger," their two marriageable daughters, Miami and Edna, and their son, Charlie, live in a village where fish, fruit, and flowers are plentiful, and where scarlet loincloths and girdles of vines suffice as clothing. Mrs. Mouth would gladly trade her prelapsarian paradise in Mediaville, however, for a villa with a water closet in the comparative metropolis of Cuna-Cuna. There, she thinks, the girls would find eligible suitors, even pursue an education at the university; and there, in her fondest dream, the family would enter society. The family does not altogether share her vision:

> In what way, [Miami] reflected, would the family gain by *entering Society,* and how did one enter it at all? There would be a gathering, doubtless, of the elect (probably armed), since the best Society is exclusive and difficult to enter. And then? Did one burrow? Or charge? She had sometimes heard it said that people "pushed" . . . and closing her eyes, Miss Miami Mouth sought to picture her parents, assisted by her small sister, Edna, and her brother, Charlie, forcing their way, perspiring but triumphant, into the highest social circles of the city of Cuna-Cuna.

But Mrs. Mouth has ultimately her way. Over her husband's protests and Miami's reluctance to leave Bamboo, her boyfriend, the family journeys to Cuna-Cuna and takes up residence in a villa owned by Madame Ruiz, the arbiter elegantiarum of Cuna-Cuna society. Naively, Mrs. Mouth considers that renting a house from such a person should carry social acceptance in its wake. "Prancing Nigger, I t'ink it bery strange dat Madame Ruiz she nebba call," she complains, and so she sends flowers to the great lady via Edna, who thereupon meets and falls in love with Madame Ruiz's rakish son, Vittorio. A subsequent earthquake, remotely traceable to Edna's and Vittorio's grand passion, devastates a local convent, prompting Madame Ruiz to open her Villa Alba for a gala evening in support of a relief fund. Seizing her chance, Mrs. Mouth descends upon the Villa with her family. Edna seizes the same occasion to disappear with Vittorio into a life of sin, and it is that night that Miami learns Bamboo was eaten by a shark on the night of the earthquake. In a final tableau that suggests the family's irreparable exile from Eden, Edna looks down from the balcony of her love nest and sees Miami marching in a religious procession, doomed by her broken heart to the penitential life of a nun and unwilling to meet her fallen sister's eyes.

If the fable of *Prancing Nigger* is timeless and sobering, the world of the novel is irrepressibly that of *The Flower Beneath the Foot.* The setting is once again a world of social competitiveness and arcane etiquette, and even in so anthropologically primitive a world, the only society is still High Society. Whatever his delights in the Gauguin myth, Firbank cannot allow that Mediaville is truly paradise—it is, rather, some midway state between the pre- and postlapsarian conditions, as the name "Mediaville" suggests. Gramophones and modern dance steps are to be found there, as well as racial snobbery and an obsequious deference to the neighbors' good opinion:

> Having broken or discarded her girdle of leaves, Miss Miami Mouth, attracted by the gramophone, appeared to be teaching a hectic two-step to the cat.
>
> "Fie, fie, my lass. Why you be so *Indian?*" her mother exclaimed, bestowing, with the full force of a carpet slipper, a well-aimed spank from behind.
>
> *"Aïe, aïe!"*
>
> "Sh'o: you nohow select!"
>
> *"Aïe. . . ."*
>
> "De low exhibition!"
>
> "I had to take off my apron, 'cos it seemed to draw de bees," Miami tearfully explained, catching up the cat in her arms.
>
> "Ob course, if you choose to wear roses. . . ."
>
> "It was but ivy!"
>
> "De berries ob de ivy entice de same," Mrs. Mouth replied, nodding graciously, from the window, to Papy Paul, the next-door neighbour, who appeared to be taking a lonely stroll with a lanthorn and a pineapple.

The language of such a passage also helps to establish Mediaville as a part of the Firbankian world. With macaronic effect, the dialectical speech is intermixed with comparatively grandiose, even elegant moral abstractions in phrases like "nohow *select,*" "de low *exhibition,*" and "de ivy *entice*" [emphasis mine]. If the mix flirts with racial offensiveness, it does so shamelessly, with no attempt to render the native patois as anything other than a racist convention.[12] Indeed, Miami's phonetically exotic *Aïe*'s mock the phonetic inconsistency of "ob de ivy," which should surely be "ob de *iby*" if Mrs. Mouth cannot manage a fricative, and her *if* should surely be *ib.* Like Firbank's slipshod spelling and grammar, and like his juxtaposition of colloquial and grandiose diction, his amateurish rendering of the patois is a surrealist technique, designed to open the reader's mind to the comic perspectives of the text—to what Kenneth Burke calls "perspective by incongruity."[13]

The world of Mediaville is also distinctly Firbank's in its sexual preoccupation. Miami's removing her apron of ivy "'cos it seemed to draw de bees" is a short, Firbankian treatise on the comparative allure of naked and seminaked bodies, and the several swarms of insects in the novel come to suggest swarms of men attracted to the Mouth girls. But in fact there are no menacing swarms of suitors for the flowerlike Miami and Edna—only Bamboo and Vittorio. The debonair Charlie and his young friends enjoy a considerably greater success than the sisters, for in Firbank's world homosexual relationships preponderate as by a law of nature. Even in Mediaville, "loosely-loinclothed" young men dance "aloofly among themselves," and Charlie pirouettes among them as heterosexual belles look on with envy. In Cuna-Cuna Mrs. Ruiz and her English companion and the archbishop and his black secretary establish a second context in which the Mouth girls have to defer to their brother's greater opportunities. "Ever so lovely are the young men of Cuna-Cuna—Juarez, Jotifa, Enid—(these, from many, to distinguish but a few)," rhapsodizes the narrator, "—but none so delicate, charming . . . as Charlie Mouth." That Charlie is entirely a free spirit in this imaginary land, even a chaser of butterflies, is Firbank's most outrageous conceit. His life goes nowhere in the story, but his sisters' lives—more under direction than his—head for tragedy: Miami, in the convent; Enid, because Vittorio is already wearying of her at the end.

Also characteristic of a Firbankian world is the mania for religion that sweeps Cuna-Cuna after the earthquake. It is no more authentically religious an impulse, of course, than Mrs. Ruiz's use of a priest's cope as a peignoir or Mr. Mouth's pious fulminations against "vanities n' innovations" when he simply opposes the move to Cuna-Cuna.

> "Intercession" services, fully choral—the latest craze of society—filled the churches . . . , sadly at the expense of other places of amusement, many of which had been obliged to close down. A religious revival was in the air, and in the Parks and streets elegant dames would stop one another in their passing carriages and pour out the stories of their iniquitous lives.

What especially distinguishes *Prancing Nigger* among the author's novels is its superimposition of this ethereal, homosexual, mock-religious, mock-bigoted, *Firbankian* world[14] upon the socially circumstanced world of Jane Austen. As Brigid Brophy has pointed out, Firbank places Austen's social unit, the family, in a tropical setting and attributes to the egregious Mrs. Mouth the great problem of all mothers in Austen novels, "namely, to balance the marriageability of daughters against their perilous seductibility."[15] Concomitantly, Mr. Mouth is a paterfamilias distinctively Austenian, a man reluctant to engage his voluble wife in conversation. When the two of them discuss the possibility of Vittorio's marrying their Edna, they might be Mr. and Mrs. Bennet discussing Elizabeth's chances with Mr. Darcy—except, of course, for the minstrel-show blackface:

> "An', to-day, honey, as I sat in de Cathedral, lis'nin' to de Archbishop, I seemed to see Edna, an' she all in *dentelles* so *chic,* comin' up de aisle, followed by twelve maids, all ob good blood, holdin' flowehs an' wid hats kimpoged ob feddehs—worn raddeh to de side, an' I heah a stranger say: 'Excuse me, sah, but who dis fine marriage?' an' a voice make reply: 'Why, dat Mr. Ruiz de million'r-'r-'r,' an' as he speak, one ob dese Italians from de Opera-house commence to sing 'De voice dat brieved o'er Eden,' an' Edna she blow a kiss at me an' laugh dat arch."
>
> "Nebba!"
>
> "Prancing Nigger, 'wait an' see'!" Mrs. Mouth waved prophetically her fan.

This Austenian world is no more than an underlay in *Prancing Nigger,* however. Like the biblical prototype of humankind's fall, it functions as a pale backdrop against which the incidental melodrama of life on Tacarigua is vividly distinguished. It is unthinkable, certainly, that Austen's characters should have their world devastated by anything so elemental as an earthquake, as it is unthinkable that the Bennet girls would go naked in public. ("No! really. De ideah!" cries Miami at the notion she should *conceal* her voluptuous body.) With no thought to immuring themselves in convents, Austen's spinsters do not even turn to religion for conventional consolation. No significant deaths occur in any of Austen's novels; no suitor, assuredly, is ingested by a shark. ("It all ober sooner dan wid de crocodile, which is some consolation for dose dat remain to mourn," reflects Mrs. Mouth upon Bamboo's death.) The measure of difference is important, for the relative temperateness of life in Jane Austen's world measures the comic extravagance of life in Firbank's world, just as the biblical Fall stands as a measure of Firbank's camping. Without crossing the line into either satire or parody, Firbank makes clear that the never-never land of his fantasy has been conceived in full consciousness of other kinds of imaginative release—that, in effect, the solaces of camp are fit to stand with those of Jane Austen and the Bible. Orchids are just the thing in a world not sufficiently orchidaceous, even the "dingy lilac blossom of rarity untold" that blooms in the gardens of the Villa Alba and whose name is *The Ronald Firbank*.

Concerning the Eccentricities of Cardinal Pirelli (1926)

Firbank's clerics are among the most libidinous in comic literature, but none of them is a more outrageous servant of the church than Don Alvaro Narciso Hernando Pirelli, cardinal-archbishop of Clemenza, and the hero of *Concerning the Eccentricities of Cardinal Pirelli.* So very outrageous are his actions that the publishers of *Prancing Nigger* rejected *Cardinal Pirelli* on both religious and moral grounds, although they must have recognized that its conceits are in many ways traditional.[16] The human failings of the protagonist are staples of Gothic fiction, after all, and the Spanish setting of the tale is in the humorous tradition of Byron, Browning, and all those English writers who have fancied that "What men call gallantry, and gods adultery, / Is much more common where the climate's sultry." As with most of his novels, Firbank finally had to publish the novel at his own expense. It appeared in bookstalls approximately five weeks after his death in 1926.

The plot of *Cardinal Pirelli* begins, perforce, with a scandal: the cardinal's sacrilegious baptism (with white crème de menthe) of the Duquesa DunEden's week-old police dog. The sacrilege is witnessed by the preposterous Monsignor Silex, a spy for the Vatican, who is less experienced in worldly matters than the cardinal and worries that the dog might be her Grace's actual progeny:

> What—disquieting doubt—if it were her Grace's offspring after all? Praise heaven, he was ignorant enough regarding the schemes of nature, but in an old lutrin once he had read of a young woman engendering a missel-thrush through the channel of her nose. It had created a good

deal of scandal to be sure at the time: the Holy Inquisition, indeed, had condemned the impudent baggage, in consequence, to the stake.

Madame Poco, the venerable superintendent of the episcopal palace, has also "crossed the borderland that divides mere curiosity from professional vigilance," and she reports to various monsignori about the cardinal's frequent indiscretions. Although the cardinal knows himself observed, he cannot restrain his appetites. His taste for every kind of experience rises above the treacherousness of Monsignor Silex and Madame Poco, however, and in the context of their venality, it seems an admirably natural exuberance:

> With the Pirelli pride, with resourceful intimacy he communed with his heart: deception is a humiliation; but humiliation is a Virtue—a Cardinal, like myself, and one of the delicate violets of our Lady's crown. . . . Incontestably, too—he had a flash of inconsequent insight, many a prod to a discourse, many a sapient thrust, delivered ex cathedrâ, amid the broken sobs of either sex, had been inspired, before now, by what prurient persons might term, perhaps, a "frolic." But away with all scruples! Once in the street in mufti, how foolish they became.
>
> The dear street. The adorable Avenidas. The quickening stimulus of the crowd: truly it was exhilarating to mingle freely with the throng!
>
> Disguised as a cabellero from the provinces or as a matron (disliking to forgo altogether the militant bravoura of a skirt), it became possible to combine philosophy, equally, with pleasure.

In a brief scene set in the Vatican, the scandals of the cardinal's public and private lives are brought to the attention of Pope Tertius II, but the narrative refocuses almost immediately upon the exotic, free-spirited denizens of Clemenza. Among them are the ever-chic Amalia Bermudez, who badgers the cathedral chapter to make a proper Christian of her blue chow in the wake of the DunEden baptism; the countess of Constantine, who is recovering from injuries sustained "while turning backward somersaults to a negro band in the black ballroom of the Infanta Eulalia-Irene"; and the poetess Diana Beira Baixa, who is rumored to have completed "a paean to her husband's '. . . .' beginning *Thou glorious wonder!*" Cardinal Pirelli, it is discovered, has fled the capital for the monastery of the Desierto. Soon he decides to flee the Iberian Peninsula altogether, but not before a midnight frolic in the dark of his cathedral with "an oncoming-looking child, with caressing liquid eyes, and a little tongue the colour of raspberry-cream." It is too much for his heart. There Madame Poco finds the cardinal dead in the morning, "dispossessed of everything but his fabulous mitre, . . . nude and elementary . . . as Adam himself." All Edens are dun, Firbank might be thought to say (in an echo of the Duquesa DunEden's suggestive name); all baptisms, mock; all sexual intriguers, doomed to Adamic dispossession.

Firbank had reason to believe in such terrible propositions,[17] but no more than in his other novels does he allow them seriously to gloss his fable. Indeed, the world he creates is so enthusiastically unprincipled, especially in matters of sexual conduct, that it makes the rigors of conventional morality seem gimcrack. His characters' thoughts about morality do not even reach syntactical completion as a rule. "Morality. Poise! For without temperance and equilibrium———," murmurs the cardinal. "For unless we have balance———," he continues, only to be distracted by a cherub's voluptuous hams. When the cardinal decides to modify his transvestite garb, it is not because he thinks that his pride in the dress is sinful (theologically, a *cardinal* sin), or thinks cross-dressing iniquitous. Rather, he fears that he would make dangerously ardent the men who molest women on the Avenue Isadora.[18]

With innocent enthusiasm, virtually everything and everyone in Clemenza invites a sexual response. Boys of "ambered paleness" and nymphomaniacal duchesses seem nature's bounty, almost God's plenty. A tower on the episcopal grounds dates from the Reformation of the Nunneries but commands "the privacy of many a drowsy [convent] patio." Oedipal and masochistic yearnings even find a dominatrix in St. Theresa of Avila, the greatest of the conventual reformers, whose ghost the cardinal encounters in the garden of the Desierto:

> She was standing by the window in the fluttered moonshine, holding a knot of whitish heliotropes.
>
> "Mother?"
>
> Saint John of the Cross could scarcely have pronounced the name with more wistful ecstasy.
>
> Worn and ill, though sublime in laughter, exquisite in tenderness, she came towards him.
>
> ". . . Child?"
>
> "Teach me, oh, teach me, dear Mother, the Way of Perfection."

The studied amorality of such scenes quashes their satiric potential—no matter the fear of Firbank's publishers that the "outspokenness of the book regarding the life of the Cardinal and particularly church matters" would inhibit sales.[19] Firbank's spoofing is altogether too silly, too empurpled, too *doting* to sustain the mood of correction essential to satire. Recognizing that the baptism of dogs has become dangerously chic, for instance, a church dignitary refuses Amalia Bermudez a baptism for her blue chow but permits her to pay for "a Mass of Intention, fully choral, *that the church may change her mind.*" It is the empurpled detail "fully choral" and the passionate italics that prevent the incident from functioning as a criticism of clerical venality. What matters venality in a church so aesthetically disposed—at least to a narrator so aesthetically partial? The occasional nun has thought herself impregnated by a demon, certainly, and convents have historically sheltered women fated by circumstances rather than by choice for a life of celibacy, but Firbank turns these sad facts into silliness with his account of a young nun in the College of the Blessed Damozels who gives herself married airs "since she had been debauched, one otiose noon, by a demon." Again, it is the empurpled details—the excessive "debauched" and the archly elegant "one otiose noon"—that conspire with the absurdity of the nun's pride to make clear the narrator's uncritical delight in her behavior.

Indeed, the narrator's attention to such behavior is the most active force in the development of the novel and functions as if it were the protagonist, exploring in a roguish and roving way the mindscape where religion, social éclat, and sexual promiscuity come together. But *exploring* is probably the wrong word; *creating* serves better, for it is an aspect of Firbank's modernism that the reader is always conscious of the disciplines of realism playing no role in the narrative. In their place are the freedoms of imagination, creativity, exaggeration. This is not to argue, of course, that realistic novels do not depend as much as the works of high modernism upon the author's creativity; only that the realistic novel must *seem* to be a transcription of the truth, and that the modernist novel, in resumed continuity with such nonrealistic novels as *Don Quixote* and *Tristram Shandy,* is permitted admissions of intervention, of serendipitous discovery, and of narrative opportunism.

Such freedoms are fundamental to Firbank's camping. The oversuffixed words in which he delights would hobble a more realistic text, but seem an absurdly elegant inlay in *Concerning the Eccentricities of Cardinal Pirelli:* "a woman . . . focusing *languishingly* upon the Cardinal," for instance; a "*gloominous* room despoiled of all splendour"; the cardinal surveying "the *preparatives* for his journey"; his face in death, "a *marvelment* to behold" [emphasis mine]. Such freedoms permit the French placing of Firbank's adverbs and adverbial phrases as near as possible to their preceding verbs with a persistently mannered, even rococo effect—permit, indeed, the multitude of strains to which Firbank submits the elasticity of English syntax in his taste for ornamental inlay. Above all, they permit whimsical excursuses into decor (an ancient fresco in the cathedral depicts "Beelzebub at Home"), into idiom ("It's time I took a toddle to know what he's about," says Madame Poco of the cardinal), and into incidents so fanciful, so entertaining, and so wry that their inlay into the text requires no justification in the plot.

The finest camp scene in the novel is the cardinal's pursuit through his cathedral of a chorister known variously theretofore as Don Sunny-locks, Don April-showers, and Don Endymion:

> Sarabandish and semi-mythic was the dance that ensued. Leading by a dozen derisive steps Don Light-of-Limb took the nave. In the dusk of the dawn it seemed to await the quickening blush of day like a white-veiled negress.
>
> "Olé, your Purpleship!"
>
> Men (eternal hunters, novelty seekers, insatiable beings), men in their natural lives, pursue the concrete no less than the ideal—qualities not seldom found combined in fairy childhood.
>
> "Olé."
>
> Oblivious of sliding mantle the Primate swooped.
>
> Up and down, in and out, round and round "the Virgin," over the worn tombed paving, through Saint Joseph, beneath the cobweb banners from Barocco to purest Moorish, by early Philip, back to Turân-Shâh—"Don't exasperate me, boy"—along the raised tribunes of the choristers and the echoing coro—the great fane (after all) was nothing but a cage; God's cage; the cage of God!

"Sarabandish and semi-mythic"? Rather, an adroitly camp interplay of the sarabandish and the sexually frenetic, the semimythic and the imperatively temporal. Sarabandish, indeed, are the interludinal parentheses and details, the arch inversions of syntax, the archaisms, and the ornate alliterations, but they function as tantalizing retards on a dance that is also a vulgar chase, coquettish on the part of the chorister, depraved on the part of the cleric, or perhaps vice versa. The chorister's *Olé*'s are cries of excited encouragement, after all, his "your Purpleship" a sauciness in the same vein, both of them stimulating the cardinal beyond his physical endurance while they heighten the churchly indecorum. Is the reader to understand the chorister's spiritedness as innocent, obscene, or amoral in the context of the churchman's half-strategic, half-desperate, wholly specious claim to some residual authority of age and dignity ("Don't exasperate me, boy") and in the context of the narrator's philosophizing about men in their natural lives pursuing the concrete no less than the ideal? The con*text* is a con*test,* ultimately—a contest of battling effects—and the orchestration of such overwrought and incompatible effects is the basic pleasure of Firbank's camp art. That the cathedral becomes climactically "a cage; God's cage; the cage of God!" suggests profundities that simply will not bear explication in a context that places questioning quotation marks around *the Virgin*.

So definitive, so purely camp, are Firbank's novels that all subsequent works of literary camp seem to defer to them, just as *Zuleika Dobson* and *Headlong Hall* seem to foreshadow them. Even in accomplished camps like E. F. Benson, P. G. Wodehouse, and Ivy Compton-Burnett, there is no scene quite so effervescently camp as the cardinal's romp with the chorister, and no flaunt to compare with Firbank's entire aestheticism. Yet a diet of Firbank, even in the short term, is very much like a diet of whipped cream. For that reason literary camp tends still—even in the wake of Firbank's achievement—to dance attendance upon farce and satire and to wed itself to such familiar genres of comedy as melodrama and the novel of manners.

5

The Novel of Histrionic Manners: E. F. Benson

The literary histories usually dismiss E. F. Benson as a "light" novelist—one prolific, but facile. He was assuredly prolific, publishing between 1893 and his death in 1940 an eight-foot shelf of books: seventy-seven works of fiction, twenty works of nonfiction, three works unclassified, and possibly a few lost plays.[1] If Benson was facile as well as prolific, he had no wish to seem so. Indeed, he regretted that the success of *Dodo,* his first novel, had encouraged him to repeat its lightness of subject and manner to the end of incapacitating himself for other modes of fiction. "Imperceptibly to myself," he wrote in his autobiography, "I had long ago reached the point at which, unless I could observe more crucially and feel more deeply, I had come to the end of anything worth saying."[2]

In an attempt to overcome his reputation for novelistic facility, Benson wrote a string of biographies, taking as his subjects Sir Francis Drake, Alcibiades, Ferdinand Magellan, Charlotte Brontë, King Edward VII, Queen Victoria, Kaiser Wilhelm II, and Queen Victoria's daughters. To his credit he consciously rejected both Victorian hagiography and the modern fashion of counting warts, preferring to write carefully researched assessments of his subjects. With the skills of a professional novelist, he turned those assessments into vivid characterization. Proudly, he records that his study of Drake moved Edmond Gosse, himself a biographer, to remark that novelists alone should be allowed to write biography.[3]

But time has proven Benson's truest gift to have been for the novelistic romp, not for judicious biography. Only the most effervescent of his hundred books survive in the bookstalls: the *Dodo* trilogy, *Paying Guests, Mrs Ames, Secret Lives,* a memoir entitled *As We Were,* a Victorian mystery novel entitled *The Luck of the Vails,* and—preeminently—a sequence of six novels known as the Lucia (or Mapp and Lucia) novels. Chronicling the adventures of Mrs. Emmeline Lucas of Riseholme, later of Tilling, and Miss Elizabeth Mapp, who has the misfortune to reign over Tilling society when Mrs. Lucas decides to replace her, the Lucia novels have enjoyed a cult status in England and America ever since their writing. Famous Luciaphils (the term and its spelling are Benson's) include Noel Coward, Gertrude Lawrence, Auberon Waugh, W. H. Auden, Nancy Mitford, and Edward Gorey. A Tilling Society, based in the Cinque Ports town of Rye, offers harbor to contemporary Luciaphils. In recent years a BBC dramatization of *Mapp and Lucia* (broadcast in the United States over PBS) and an omnibus publication of the complete novels have broadened the base of devotees.[4] Benson would have been unhappy to think it, but the Lucia novels constitute his most enduring legacy. They also constitute a high point of camp.

Queen Lucia (1920)

The Mapp and Lucia chronicles begin with *Queen Lucia,* which introduces the reader to Mrs. Emmeline Lucas, the arbiter elegantiarum of Riseholme society. As by divine right, she arranges the entertainments and cultural education of her neighbors from an Elizabethan cottage called The Hurst, an apogee of quaintness so aggressively period that the new windows proclaim their newness by looking much older than the original. Her subjects know her as Lucia—*La Lucia,* the wife of Lucas, pronounced in the Italian manner—and she encourages a general belief that she is fluent in Italian by peppering her speech with phrases in that language and by referring to her husband, Philip, as Peppino.[5] She rules her subjects, the reader is told,

> with a secure autocracy pleasant to contemplate at a time when thrones were toppling, and imperial crowns whirling like dead leaves down the autumn winds. The ruler of Riseholme, happier than he of Russia, had no need to fear the finger of Bolshevism writing on the wall, for there was not in the whole of that vat, which seethed so pleasantly with culture, one bubble of revolutionary ferment.

Actually, revolt bubbles merrily in Lucia's kingdom. Daisy Quantock, a neighbor, longs to displace her as the doyenne of village life, and to that end she brings an Indian fakir and a Russian medium to the village as if she were sponsoring royalty. Indeed, the medium, whose name is Marie Lowenstein, claims to be the Princess Popoffski. Lucia is irritated by Daisy's effrontery but manages to enlist the fakir under her own banner. Daisy is more careful to protect the princess from Lucia than the fakir, and Lucia is shortly aghast to find Riseholme transforming itself into "a spiritualistic republic, with the Princess as priestess and Mrs. Quantock as president."

More serious even than Daisy's revolt is the defection of Georgie Pillson from the role of Lucia's gentleman-in-waiting. A mature bachelor of no clear sexual orientation, Georgie is by nature a courtier but dreams secretly of being king of Riseholme. When the prima donna Olga Bracely buys a house in the village, he is asexually smitten. The spirit of Bolshevism runs amok as he throws off Lucia's authority to give Olga his timid heart, and Lucia's authority is dangerously rocked when Olga proceeds to entertain Riseholme at soirees more amusing than her own. Like a guest at Balthazar's feast, Lucia perceives the finger of doom writing on the walls about the division of her kingdom. "There was only one lawgiver in Riseholme," she has to remind herself, "one court of appeal, one dispenser of destiny."

A series of tactical mistakes loosens Lucia's hold on her rule as the novel goes on. When Georgie's sisters visit him and meet the fakir, they expose him as a waiter in a London restaurant. Ignominiously, Lucia has to return him to Daisy's camp and habituate herself to refer not to *her* guru but to *poor Daisy*'s guru. On another occasion, she is seated at Olga's dinner table next to a distinguished Italian composer named Cortese and has cause to wish she had never affected knowledge of Italian. Her pretense to musical erudition serves her no better than her rudimentary Italian when Olga hires the Spanish Quartet to play in Riseholme. Lucia forms the impression that they are a local group that plays in a Brinton hotel and attempts some gentle one-upmanship. "I know one ought never to compare, but have you ever heard the Spanish Quartet, Miss Bracely?" she inquires sweetly. "In that fell moment," one is told, "the Bolshevists laid bony fingers on the scepter of her musical autocracy."

That only Olga is *without* Bolshevist design on Lucia's power is the central irony of the novel. Inhabiting a world much larger than Riseholme, Olga has no need to rule locally. At the end she sends Georgie back to Lucia while keeping what there is of his heart as she departs for a concert tour in America. To Lucia's relief, the Princess Popoffski disappears as well, to reappear in a newspaper when brought up in court and charged with fraud. These troubling outsiders dispersed and the Bolshevist aberrations of her subjects quashed—with a fine sense that she has preserved her monarchy—Lucia rules Riseholme once again.

As this summary suggests, *Queen Lucia* is a comedy of village manners, with a line clearly drawn between insiders and outsiders. References to Bolshevism and revolutionary outrages may seem to suggest that Riseholme is something more than a village—a microcosm, even, of beleaguered monarchies the world over—but one is never permitted to take seriously that analogy. Indeed, Riseholme is essentially a stage set, not a sociopolitical entity. It is modeled in part on Stratford-upon-Avon, and like that elaborate stage set, it treasures an Elizabethan heritage as a commercially useful identity.[6] Lucia sets the general tone of the place in her happiness to suffer the inconvenience of an Elizabethan spit in her fireplace and a parlor so dark that to read in it is impossible. The ghost of Shakespeare wandering in her garden would never detect the modern doorbell artfully concealed in an antique bellpull, and he would be gratified, she likes to think, by the sight of borders consisting solely of flowers named by Perdita and Ophelia.

Indeed, so thoroughly contrived is Riseholme as a mise-en-scène that little in the town is simply what it seems. The Ambermere Arms is a hotel that serves covertly as an antique shop, and a printing shop at Ye Signe of ye Daffodille specializes in typography unreadably Elizabethan although it is a new establishment, set up by the Lucases to serve Peppino as a vanity press. What would pass in any other village for a duck pond is in Riseholme a dunking pond, with stocks purchased from another town set suggestively on its shore to further the deception. Lucia and her circle take the lead in this municipal chicanery. The autocratic Lady Ambermere rules the town socially to all appearances, but untitled Lucia outranks her in every way that matters. Neither Georgie nor Lucia admit to wearing eyeglasses in private or to practicing beforehand the piano duets that they pretend to sight-read together. "Now, mustn't scold," Lucia is fond of scolding her potential critics in elaborately inflected baby talk—as if someone would dare. So heady, so hypertrophied, so egregiously camp is the air of theater in Riseholme that Daisy's fakir and Miss Lowenstein might be thought to gravitate there naturally.

This theatricalism is particularly evident in the Riseholme mode of conversation, which is less a process of shared communication than a drama of one-upmanship in which each actor is his or her own best audience. Mrs. Weston confides to Georgie her deduction that Olga Bracely has decided to settle in Riseholme, but she does so only because she is "convinced that nobody else had put two and two together with the same brilliant result as herself." Meanwhile, Georgie delights "in the even superior position of having known the result without having to do any addition at all." The Italian phrases that Lucia, Peppino, and Georgie affect are similarly theatrical—restricted to stagy greetings and exclamations for the most part, and useless in real conversation. Tête-à-têtes are encouraged at The Hurst through such elaborately contrived illusions as a china canary in a Chippendale cage and a make-believe spider in a silk web, apparently on the principle that artifice breeds artifice. Lucia has even thought of writing an essay to be entitled "The Gambits of Conversation Derived from Furniture." The bewildering profusion of mottoes in Riseholme's gardens is an overflow of this staginess. "*Tempus fugit,*" cries a sundial at The Hurst; "Bide a wee," contradicts a nearby resting place; "Much have I travelled in the realms of gold," avers a rustic bench.

If Riseholme is a stage, Lucia is without question its most illustrious actress. "Indeed, she did not usually stop at taking the leading part," one is told, "but, if possible, doubled another character with it, as well as being stage manager and adapter, if not designer of scenery. Whatever she did . . . she did it with all the might of her dramatic perception, did it in fact with such earnestness that she had no time to have an eye to the gallery at all; she simply contemplated herself and her own vigorous accomplishment." This histrionic instinct inspires her to arrange "thrills of pleasant excitement and conjectural exercise" for Riseholme, as when she allows luggage to arrive without her at The Hurst. She herself walks slowly from the train station, delaying her entrance in the tradition of star performers. Her romantic dalliance with Georgie is another theatrical ploy, an illusion offering mystery and a whiff of possible scandal to her public. Always the actress, she holds her head carefully in profile against the dark walls of her music room as she plays the slow movement of the *Moonlight* sonata for her guests, entrancing herself with what she conceives to be the exquisite pathos of her performance and appearance.

That everyone sees through Lucia's performance does not diminish her power or make her ridiculous in a town where artifice is the accepted norm, for it is performance qua performance that earns respect in Riseholme, in accordance with the camp taste. Everyone knows that Lucia cannot manage intricacies in the faster movements of the *Moonlight* sonata, yet when she stops at the end of the slow movement, closes her piano, and murmurs regretfully that the other movements are "more like morning and afternoon," she is capable of wiping genuine moisture from her eyes. *No one* dare guffaw. Similarly, it is generally known that Georgie wears a toupee and colors his hair, but Georgie carries on as if his secret were secure, and for that reason the Riseholmites have no impulse to shatter the illusion with laughter. Daisy Quantock will sometimes resort to sarcasm in an effort to break through Lucia's pretense and speak the plain truth, but Lucia can always defeat her with a deadlier weapon—dissembled unconsciousness of there having been a sarcasm.

If Lucia has a meaningful antagonist, it is not the demon of imposture that goads her into increasingly ambitious roles, then. Overreaching is generally respected in Riseholme as a manifestation of theatrical courage. Nor is her enemy a person who would tell the truth straightforwardly. Daisy is only pestiferous in that regard. Lucia's truest enemy is Olga, a woman who is everything that Lucia pretends to be and who threatens to supplant a queenship based on artifice with claims of real achievement. An accomplished musician and a competent linguist, Olga is also a thoroughly good person. She never betrays Lucia's ignorance of music and languages; she refuses to encourage Georgie's defection from The Hurst; and she absents herself from Riseholme whenever her natural affability threatens to bring down Lucia's rule. But from Lucia's point of view she is maddening—a plain-dealing marplot in the high drama of village life. However eminent in the great world and however great her talent, Olga is naive about life as it must be enlivened in an English village. There, tedium *has* to be relieved by a playacting that makes acceptably genteel the general greed for money, news, and reputation.

Readers tend to agree with Lucia that Olga is a marplot not only because they enjoy the opera buffa of life in Riseholme but because Olga herself respects the alchemy of transformation. In a more conventional, moralistic comedy, Olga would be the naïf who cries out commonsensically that the queen of Riseholme wears no clothes. But Olga makes no attempt to expose Lucia's nakedness. A professional illusionist herself, she even delights in the sheer nerve with which Lucia spins her invisible robes out of nonexistent graces. Benson's camp assumption and Olga's tacit admission is that life is made agreeable by such camp artifice. Lucia's duplicity is never allowed to become a moral issue.

Lucia's pretensions are even a kind of public service. Certainly she has no intention to misinform when she opines recklessly that Wagner knew nothing of dramatic effects or that Shakespeare knew nothing of institutions for the mentally insane. She has only a wish to appear knowledgeable and to heighten cultural awareness. Would a stable monarchy be well served by anything less? Boldly, she will risk a complete exposure of her pretensions to culture to keep alive the illusion that the queen does not go naked. After the fiasco of trying to speak Italian to Signor Cortese, for instance, she listens to a song recital, her mind "furiously busy as to how to make anything whatever out of so bad a job," her face wearing a carefully enraptured expression. Her ingenious solution is to announce that Cortese's accent is Neapolitan, vulgar, and impenetrable to lovers of *la bella lingua*. "He had not an 'h' when he spoke English, and I have not the slightest doubt in my own mind that his Italian was equally illiterate," she assures Georgie, who *knows* she is overreaching. Audaciously, she raises the stakes: "It does not matter; I do not see that Mr. Cortese's linguistic accomplishments concern us. But his music does, if poor Miss Bracely, with her lovely notes, is going to study it, and appear as Lucretia. I am sorry if that is so." Blithely, she puts it all behind her and queries, "Any news?" as if her own exposure were not the main news of the day.

Is a ruler with such personal style to be overthrown for Lady Ambermere, a woman thrown into confusion by a simple snub? Is she to be overthrown in the name of honest dealings for Olga, who is forever an outsider in Riseholme, off at any moment to America or the continent? Shall Daisy, who is unable even to retain the allegiance of her guru, rule in Lucia's stead? Shall Georgie, so entirely and absurdly a gentleman-in-waiting? Lucia is everything that her critics charge—arrogant, epicene, ridiculous, pretentious, a sham—but she is also stylish and vital, an altogether rococo achievement of her own imagination that enables Riseholme to bubble merrily with gossip, speculation, and intrigue. The camp taste could wish for nothing more.

Miss Mapp (1922)

With *Miss Mapp,* the mise-en-scène of the *Mapp and Lucia* series shifts from Riseholme to Tilling—instantly recognizable as the Cinque Ports town of Rye. From a house named Mallards, Miss Elizabeth Mapp attempts to dominate the town in the same way Lucia reigns over Riseholme from The Hurst. But Mapp is a woman of "malignant curiosity" and "cancerous suspicions," and her bad nature boils too close to the surface for valid comparison with Lucia's more subtle and sugarcoated nature. Indeed, Mapp's capacity for rage is unsurpassed in a town where, Benson tells us, rage is the only passion. Captain Richard Puffin and Major Benjamin Flint, her neighbors, have "hurricane" tempers that storm whenever one man loses a golf match to the other, and to the horror of both men a question of who-is-drinking-more-of-whose-whiskey nearly results in a duel. The beginning of daylight saving time in Tilling inspires such heated controversy that the Reverend Bartlett ("Padre") feels compelled to preach a sermon on Christian forbearance. When Diva Plaistow purchases a length of worsted wool that Mapp had intended to purchase for herself, Mapp is pitiless in her revenge. Millinery war is declared, and appliquéd flowers and vats of crimson dye are thrown recklessly into the fray. In Tilling, the reader is told, even cardgames are blood sport.

This violence of interpersonal feeling and the accommodations to social necessity that keep it in check are the novel's continual focus. Susan Poppit is in Mapp's eyes an obnoxious climber whose social ambition is as offensively great as her bosom. When Susan is made a Member of the British Empire, Mapp is contemptuous, but when that honor is followed by the romantic attentions of the town's preeminent bachelor, Algernon Wyse, Mapp is forced to acknowledge Susan socially. Trying to rival Susan's romantic appeal, Mapp thereupon spreads rumors that she herself was the cause of the duel almost staged by the major and the captain. The consequences of her rumors are dizzying: Mapp discovers that the gentlemen are secret tipplers; they blackmail her into silence by threatening to say they found her drunk on the street; she discovers and broadcasts the fact that both men backed off from the duel; they sue for peace; she forgives only the major, thus driving a wedge between the friends. Finally Captain Puffin suffers a stroke at his dinner table and drowns in a bowl of soup, leaving the major to turn to Miss Mapp in his loneliness, exactly as she would have had it from the beginning. In another relationship, an obbligato to these events, Mapp has to grant social recognition to Irene Coles, a talented young artist who is apparently lesbian. Mapp would gladly snub "quaint" Irene were she not afraid of the woman's gift for devastating candor. Social life in Tilling is a jumble of just such cross-vectored relationships.

Benson did not have a series clearly in mind when he followed *Queen Lucia* with *Miss Mapp*. The inspiration of the later work was the view from his own windows of the ladies of Rye doing their shopping in the High Street each morning and finding a great deal to say to each other. He recalled in his autobiography that he began gradually to imagine "an elderly atrocious spinster" who would observe the High Street from those windows in his own home:

> She should be the centre of social life, abhorred and dominant, and she should sit like a great spider behind the curtains in the garden-room, spying on her friends, and I knew that her name must be Elizabeth Mapp. Rye should furnish the topography, so that none could mistake where the scene was laid, and this should be the busy little town called Tilling.

But the possibility of a confrontation betwen Mapp and Lucia was always a possibility:

> Perhaps another preposterous woman, Lucia of Riseholme, who already had a decent and devout following, and who was as dominant as Mapp, might come into contact with her some day, when I got to know Mapp better. I began to invent a new set of characters who should revolve round these two women, fussy and eager and alert and preposterous. Of course, it would all be small beer, but one could get a head upon it of jealousies and malignities and devouring inquisitiveness. Like Moses on Pisgah, I saw a wide prospect, a Promised Land, a Saga indefinitely unveiling itself. But one had to get a firm hold of Elizabeth Mapp first. Lucia I knew.[7]

The terms in which Benson speaks of Mapp—"an elderly atrocious spinster," "abhorred and dominant"—suggest a darkening of his comic palette in the transposition from Riseholme to Tilling. Quarrels are "meat and drink" to Mapp, we are told, and she is a woman of large appetite who enjoys disputing with tradesmen almost as much as faulting the Padre's grammar. Instinctively duplicitous, she finds it "very inconvenient that honesty should be the best policy." No revenge is too petty for her to undertake;

no advantage, too mean to seize. When Isabel Poppit invites her belatedly to a card party, Mapp deduces immediately that she is to take the place of some preferred guest who declined at the last minute. Her revenge, precisely calculated, is to promise to look in *if she can,* leaving Isabel exquisitely uncertain of the number for her tables.

Such calculations make Mapp the dark center of events in Tilling. Not merely a "trained observer of the street," she is also a logician, devoted to facts, "incapable of believing the improbable," and fearsomely determined that no one shall ever get away with anything. She is aware that she has never actually caught the Reverend Bartlett cheating at cards but retains her suspicions, and she puzzles nightly over the relationship between Captain Puffin and Major Flint until she has got it right. When Susan Poppit and Algernon Wyse begin to keep company, she is an implacable spy, all the more dangerous because she does not mistake her salacious fantasies for hard evidence:

> It was easier to imagine the worst, and she had already pictured to herself a clandestine meeting between those passionate ones, who under cover of this darkness were imperviously concealed from any observation (beneath an umbrella) from her house roof. Nothing but a powerful searchlight could reveal what was going on in the drawing-room window of Mr. Wyse's house, and apart from the fact that she had not got a powerful searchlight, it was strongly improbable that anything of a very intimate nature was going on there . . . it was not likely that they would choose the drawing-room window. She thought of calling on Mr. Wyse and asking for the loan of a book, so that she would see whether the sables were in the hall, but even then she would not really be much further on.

Elaborate schemes for putting people in their place also occupy Mapp greatly. She goes to a garden party with the plan of tasting one spoonful of red-currant fool, crying, "Delicious!" and leaving the rest uneaten. She likes very much on such social occasions to collect all the men about her and then scold them for not talking to the other ladies. Maliciously, she suggests to Diva that she will be in trouble with the authorities for hoarding coal. There is, in fact, no rationing, and Mapp herself is hoarding not only coal but food.

Mapp's appalling meanness of spirit makes her a very different sort of study from Lucia. Lucia is an enchantress who creates a make-believe world of art and culture in a wasteland of the spirit, whereas Mapp is a Boeotian who spreads darkness of spirit from some inexhaustible core of malignity within her. Benson's joke is that Mapp fancies herself a Lucia and works as hard as Lucia at her queenship of Tilling. To a superficial observer, she seems "a rollicking good-natured figure of a woman." She showers smiles and bows upon her acquaintances and affects an enthusiasm for all things bright and beautiful—for the "sweet" stars (her gushing is endless), for the butterflies frolicking so happily in her garden (they are always happier in her garden than in other gardens, it seems), and for "quaint" Irene (whom she loathes). But those who know Mapp at all know the truth. Her acuteness of hearing is one of the local terrors, and vengeance has for her "a concentrated sweetness as of saccharin contrasted with ordinary lump sugar." As the sun streaming through windows in the church stains her face all colors on Christmas morning, she sings about Peace on Earth and imagines that the other worshipers see her in a sort of celestial radiance. She would be shocked that Diva, sitting opposite, is reminded of the iridescent hues on cold beef.

Taking their cue from Mapp as if she were a source of infection, the other Tillingites are quicker to take revenge, more eager to quarrel, and more nasty in their calculations than the comparatively sweet-natured Riseholmites. Diva, for instance, is fond of the stinging rejoinder that is "short, swift, and spontaneous." She is equally fond of the stinging gesture. With impeccable calculation, she revenges herself upon Mapp for copying her new dress by arranging for her maid to wear the original dress and to confront Mapp, dressed in the copy, in view of all Tilling. No less given to stage effects, the Reverend Bartlett feigns sweet eccentricity in the affectation of a preposterous Highland idiom, but one has glimpses of domestic tyranny in the parsonage. Under their charade of camaraderie, the major and captain cordially despise each other, the captain regarding the major as a boor, the major thinking the captain effete. Neither can bear to lose points to the other at golf or in argument, and their bad behavior in defeat is as predictable as it is ghastly. Games of any kind strip the veneer from Tilling society, for they liberate hostilities onto an acceptable battlefield:

All semblance of manners was invariably thrown to the winds by the ladies of Tilling when once bridge began; primeval hatred took their place. The winners of any hand were exasperatingly condescending to the losers, and the losers correspondingly bitter and tremulous. Miss Mapp failed to get her contract, as her partner's contribution to success consisted of more twos and threes than were ever seen together before, and when quaint Irene at the end said, "Bad luck, Mapp," Miss Mapp's hands trembled so much with passion that she with difficulty marked the score. But she could command her voice sufficiently to say, "Lovely of you to be sympathetic, dear." Irene in answer gave a short, hoarse laugh and dealt.

Mapp may be less skilled than Lucia as an actress and the Tillingites may be cruder of soul than the Riseholmites, but Benson's two casts of characters are otherwise very similar. Things are simply more blatant in Tilling than in Riseholme—the hostilities more open, the playacting more obvious. If Mapp is a variation of Lucia, Diva Plaistow is her Daisy; the major, her Georgie; the Contessa Faraglione (sister of Algernon Wyse), her Olga. All these secondary characters are more grotesque than their counterparts in *Queen Lucia* but arrayed in similar fashion about a woman whose passion for superintending society keeps their relations at a boil. The occasional iteration of a phrase underscores the similarities. Like Lucia, Mapp is fond of telling people not to scold her, and she has even adopted "au reservoir," Lucia's witticism for au revoir, as her own.[8]

The echoing of *Queen Lucia* in *Miss Mapp* was not intended to parody the successful formula of the earlier novel but to reduce its drama of social hypocrisy to terms not blurred by Lucia's charm and Riseholme's warm heart. Benson is clearer in the later novel that it is not hypocrisy but the circumscription of village life that compels people to observe the basic tenets of civilization. "If quarrels were permanent in Tilling," he observes, "nobody would be on speaking terms any more with anyone else in a day or two." It follows that civilized reconciliations are necessary, however hypocritical they may seem. But a consequence hardly less disastrous, he argues, is that there could be no *fresh* quarrels with anyone. That outrageous contention that good behavior is valuable because it allows scope to bad behavior is the capstone of his classically camp conceit that human conduct transpires on a stage, that the only real values are dramatic, and that conflicts are more dramatically interesting than amity.

The whole giddy argument invites readers to transcend hypocrisy and admit that they treasure the bad behavior of Benson's characters at the same time that their laughter rebukes such failings.

Benson compels the readers of *Miss Mapp* to recognize a morally anarchic principle at work in their delight—the same principle at work in the machinations of the Tillingites. If one thrills with anticipation at the end of the novel when Mapp reflects that Major Benjy will be lonely after Captain Puffin's death, it is because one senses that her implied solicitude makes possible a matrimonial ambition so chilling from all points of view that she could not otherwise entertain it. One cares nothing for Major Benjy's vulnerability or for Mapp's soul, for Benson has seduced his readers into a point of view that understands all creatures as naturally predacious and all systems of logic and morality as the accommodations of outraged human sensibility. It is the same point of view encouraged by the literary naturalists, of course, but camp in Benson's novel—as frivolous as it is serious. That note of frivolity is perfectly caught in an epilogue both terrible and wickedly funny—a pastiche of natural predaciousness, mock empathy, and pleasantries run amok:

> It was a warm, bright day of February, and a butterfly was enjoying itself in the pale sunshine on the other window, and perhaps (so Miss Mapp sympathetically interpreted its feelings) was rather annoyed that it could not fly away through the pane. It was not a white butterfly, but a tortoiseshell, very pretty, and in order to let it enjoy itself more, she opened the window, and it fluttered out into the garden. Before it had flown many yards, a starling ate most of it up, so the starling enjoyed itself, too.

Lucia in London (1927)

In *Lucia in London,* the mise-en-scène of the Mapp and Lucia sequence shifts once again. A legacy from a remote aunt allows Lucia and Peppino to establish residence in Brompton Square, whereupon Lucia lays siege to London society with her accustomed vigor. Riseholme seethes with offended feelings in the background, but Lucia has an eye on greater things, and she gathers around her a new group of friends. Among them are Aggie Sandeman, who opens the door to society for her; Adele Brixton, a fellow social climber, *Lord* Tony Limpsfield, a great catch; and Stephen Merriall, who is invaluable to her in his secret life as Hermione, the author of a society column. Gradually there evolves a secret society in London that calls itself the Luciaphils, membership in which is based on unapproving but bedazzled admiration of Lucia's temerity. Like a woman possessed, she throws both caution and credibility to the wind in a number of social gambits. She curtsies to the telephone at the end of a conversation with Peppino to suggest to her guests that royalty had called. She affects that Stephen Merriall is her secret lover, hoping desperately that he will not mistake the ploy for flirtation. She crashes shamelessly the parties of titled persons, lurking in the street to intercept a hostess if need be, no effrontery too great when a duchess is her prey.

The whole endeavor crashes suddenly to a halt when Peppino becomes seriously ill, exhausted by the pace Lucia has set him in London. With barely a regret, Lucia returns with him immediately to Riseholme, where she nurses him devotedly while setting about the repair of her tattered queenship. To that end, she conjures a spook named Vittoria at her ouija board to upstage a spook named Abfu that Daisy had made briefly popular, and Fate lends her a hand when a museum of local history that Daisy and Georgie had the effrontery to organize in her absence burns conveniently to the ground. With a comfortable sigh, Riseholme settles down under the restored monarchy. The creative energy of Lucia's siege of London is thrown into relief by this easy restoration of the old order, and her London enterprise is more clearly in retrospect what it seemed at the time: a kind of delirium, a fever finally broken at the end.

The fun of the novel and its camp appeal is that the delirium of Lucia's runaway ambition never bedims her sense of genteel propriety. All the while that she seems wildly out of control she is also calculating minutiae of etiquette and decorum, and the two behaviors are a giddy counterpoint. If she embraces recklessly the music of Stravinsky because it is fashionable in London, she graciously modulates her condescension toward those bewildered by *Le sacre du printemps* as she plays it for them neglecting totally the intricate shifts of key. The magnitude of Auntie's bequest requires a proportional show of grief, she thinks, and good taste dictates a reluctance to mention details of wealth. Thus, she can permit details of the inheritance to escape her only in discreet measure although she is as purse-proud as Midas and eager to broadcast her news. In conversation with Georgie, she notes first the vulgarity of people's curiosity about the inheritance, then permits herself an admission that one's dear friends have an understandable interest. Consideration follows of the social responsibilities that accompany great wealth, succeeded by a small list of expenditures she might now permit herself. Then she mentions coyly a duty to the house in Brompton Square where Dear Auntie was born. By the time the measured revelations are over and the flow of pieties is exhausted, Georgie has calculated the inheritance accurately at three thousand pounds a year.

And that is the final joke—that through all the stately indirection of Lucia's discourse, Georgie is calculating as madly as she, the two of them caught up in a formal exercise of manners as stylized as a minuet but with a level of important communication. On arriving home, Georgie sees Daisy waiting at her bedroom window for a report and calls across, "Three thousand," not needing to preface the words with an explanation, so perfect is Daisy's understanding that an accurate calculation of the Lucases' inheritance is of interest beyond all consideration of manners. "No!" says Daisy. As if caught up in this drama of endless calculation, the narrator proceeds to calculate precisely the meaning of Daisy's *No:*

> This simple word "No" connoted a great deal in the Riseholme vernacular. It was used, of course, as a mere negative, without emphasis, and if you wanted to give weight to your negative, you added "Certainly not." But when you used the word "No" with emphasis, as Daisy had used it from her bedroom window to Georgie, it was not a negative at all, and its signification briefly put was "I never heard anything so marvellous, and it thrills me through and through. Please go on at once, and tell me a great deal more, and then let us talk it all over."

The effect of such incessant calculation and cross-calculation of effects is to suggest a world so deeply mannered that all social intercourse is a code, as in the novel of manners. Yet it is not the large world that is encoded, only Lucia's world, for the Luciaphils act straightforwardly enough in London, and Olga is a notoriously plain speaker in Riseholme. The difference is that Olga is an outsider in Lucia's world of pretense, and Lucia is an outsider in London, no longer an orchestrator of illusions. Carrying her own world with her like a carapace, she seems exotic to Londoners, even slightly mad. They boggle when she envies the notoriety of a woman involved in a sex scandal and begins a campaign of sly hints that Stephen Merriall is her lover. The Riseholmites have seen the sterile exercise before, of course—with Georgie. What sane purpose is served by its reprise in London? She strikes profound fear in Merriall's unmanly breast until he grasps her game, and she vastly amuses the Luciaphils, who are not deceived for a moment. The charade becomes farce when she mistakes her bedroom door in a country house and enters Merriall's room in dishabille. *He* is all outraged virtue; *she* is all outraged virtue. Their curious problem is how to dramatize their outrage when they are already playing at lost innocence.

Yet to judge Lucia insane or foolish would be crude. The affectations that never fool anyone, the extraordinary expenditure of energy upon evanescent goals, and the willingness to risk all her dramatic effects upon a momentary inspiration make her an actress, not a Madwoman of Chaillot. She is an actress with only a middling talent, perhaps, and suited better to the provincial stage than to the London, but she has the confidence of a great actress in her ability to bring off a scene. Audiences respond appropriately to her camp appeal, pleasurably appalled by her vulgarity but moved by her indomitable spirit, delighted equally by the flaws of her performance and by its great daring. Indeed, on the few occasions when facts supplant illusion in her performance, the audience complains. Daisy is acutely disappointed to add up all the accounts of dinner parties and musical evenings chronicled in Hermione's column and discover that Lucia had not actually spent more evenings in London society than the season provided. She is indignant that Lucia feigns grief for Peppino's aunt, of course, but not disappointed in any sense. Like everyone in Riseholme and like almost everyone in London, she finds Lucia to be outrageous so that she *can* experience indignation.

In no other novel in the Mapp and Lucia sequence does the reader see Lucia so much from the point of view of her audience. And in no other novel is Benson so clear that her audience needs Lucia, if only for her ability to render the trivialities of life intense for others. Georgie is deeply hurt when his queen chooses London over Riseholme and resolves to have nothing more to do with her, but he has soon to admit to himself that life without Lucia is without tonic:

However much he told himself he did not want her, he like all the rest of Riseholme was beginning to miss her dreadfully. She aggravated and exasperated them; she was a hypocrite (all that pretence of not having read the Mozart duet, and desolation at Auntie's death), a poseuse, a sham, and a snob, but there was something about her that stirred you into violent though protesting activity, and though she might infuriate you, she prevented your being dull.

Mapp and Lucia (1931)

Lucia is a recent widow at the beginning of *Mapp and Lucia,* Peppino having expired in the interim between novels. During her period of deepest mourning, she had had to surrender to Daisy the control of an Elizabethan pageant she had planned for the village, and as she begins to throw off her widow's weeds she discovers that Daisy intends to keep control. Such arrant lese majesty requires that Lucia absent herself from Riseholme until the pageant is over. Mapp has advertised for a tenant, so Lucia rents Mallards for the summer and inveigles Georgie to rent an adjoining cottage. Mapp remains on the scene, however, for Tilling has a trickle-down economy: she rents Diva's house; Diva, Irene's house; Irene, a laborer's cottage. Mapp intends that her tenant, whom she styles *Lulu,* shall not be too popular. "She wanted to have Lucia in her pocket," the reader is told, "to take her by the hand and show her to Tilling, but to be in control." Lucia has other ideas, and to Mapp's fury she sets out to be queen of Tilling via large doses of charm. Success follows upon success. She even finds time to return briefly to Riseholme and salvage the pageant when Daisy's generalship falls apart.

Increasingly impolite skirmishes between Mapp and Lucia rapidly absorb Tilling. Because she is paying his salary, Lucia contravenes Mapp's orders to her gardener. Mapp bursts into Mallards without knocking, so Lucia puts the door on a chain that Mapp impatiently snaps. Against Mapp's explicit orders, Lucia permits a charity fete in Mallard's gardens, and as chairwoman of a municipal art exhibit, Mapp treats canvases by Lucia and Georgie to summary rejection. "Is it war?" Georgie asks with each new confrontation. The real issue, Mapp insists, is if England is a free country under Lucia. Lucia resolves to teach Mapp her manners—if she is not too old to learn. When Lucia decides to settle permanently in Tilling in a house called Grebe, Irene looks forward to Mapp's hearing the news: "I must be there when she's told. She'll say, 'Darling Lulu, what a joy,' and then fall down and foam at the mouth."

In an unexpected development, a sudden flood sets Mapp and Lucia adrift on the high seas atop a kitchen table, and they are presumed dead. Georgie is Lucia's heir; Major Benjy, Mapp's. Georgie proceeds cautiously to claim his inheritance; the major, precipitously. When the ladies reappear after several months' absence, having been saved by Italian fishermen, Mapp finds the major cozily settled in Mallards. Her initial fury is as great as her temporary stink of cod, but when the major tries to appease her with an offer of marriage, she sees a way to upstage Lucia by writing a new chapter in the book of pardon. She turns to Lucia when the banns are announced in church and can barely refrain from sticking out her tongue.

It is one of the pleasures of the Mapp and Lucia sequence that in each novel Benson sets himself a different focus: village life as innocent theater in *Queen Lucia;* the malignity of village manners in *Miss Mapp;* the needs of audiences in *Lucia in London.* With *Mapp and Lucia,* he brings together these several theatrical strands and stages a battle of leading ladies. It is his best novel largely because Mapp and Lucia have worthy competition for the first time. Daisy is never really competition for Lucia, for her efforts to supplant Lucia collapse of their own inadequacy, and Diva has no taste for competition with Mapp, only a sense of personal dignity that goads her into occasional self-defense. Georgie is capable of gentle rebellion but is generally Lucia's lapdog. Susan Wyse, Lady Ambermere, Major Benjy, Captain Puffin, the Padre—all are ninepins before Mapp's or Lucia's resolve. Quaint Irene might offer the ladies a challenge, but she laughs at Mapp and worships Lucia blindly.

The competition between Mapp and Lucia is so generally equitable, on the other hand, that neither can sustain an advantage. If Lucia is always able to reverse Mapp's victories, Mapp never tires of dealing Lucia some fresh blow, usually from an unexpected quarter. They know each other completely. Lucia is never deceived by the grisly sweetness that Mapp affects—"Dearest Lulu" and that sort of thing—and Mapp never underestimates Lucia's implacable ambition. Their quid pro quos suggest deeper, connatural reciprocities, as when each does a public imitation of the other, each meaning by the cruel burlesque to declare total war between them. Differences only aggravate their rivalry. Competition flares into antagonism largely because Lucia is more intelligent and a better actress than Mapp and because Mapp can draw upon reserves of wrath and ill temper that Lucia does not possess.

In pitting Mapp and Lucia against each other, Benson provided each woman with a new world to conquer but at the same time increased the difficulties in her way. The result is a narrative line extravagantly camp—rich with reversals and clotted with fine, ironic moments. When Lucia's musical evenings grow tedious, for instance, Mapp initiates a resistance movement among the guests and has very nearly organized a boycott when Mr. Wyse announces that he will bring the Contessa Faraglione to one of the evenings for the pleasure of hearing Lucia speak Italian. Certain that Lucia cannot really speak the language, Mapp immediately changes tactics and insists everyone attend the exposure. Lucia, of course, is appalled. Knowing she must under no circumstances meet the Contessa, she feigns a case of influenza and resolves with Georgie to avoid further use of their Italian tags. "It's odd," she comments wearily, "that we have to break ourselves of the habit of doing something we can't do." Mapp is not deceived, of course, and after spying upon Mallard's enclosed garden from the church tower, she has evidence that Lucia is entirely healthy—evidence that she is just ready to produce at a luncheon for the Contessa when a note from Lucia arrives couched in *exquisite* Italian. If momentarily stymied, Mapp keeps alive a hope to prove the note a fake, for every denouement is provisional in the world of *Mapp and Lucia;* every triumph, a momentary stay against the exposure of one's deceits.

The sense that no seizing of advantage or small deceit is ever abandoned by Tilling's collective consciousness is one of the best conceits of the novel. When Lucia and Georgie first visit the town they see Diva wearing the dress that Mapp copied in *Miss Mapp,* as if that symbol of factional life in the town wanted to generate its own, gossipy announcement. Formidable gossips themselves, the Tillingites expend an enormous amount of time turning over the evidence in any contretemps that catches their fancy—facts as to who was observed speaking with whom, what was asserted on what occasion—and the evidence is replayed in multiple conversations with the effect of return matches in some ongoing game of intellection. The economy of allusion in the town is simply a marvel. Nothing goes unnoticed, unremarked, or unremembered, and every development remains under intense scrutiny until it gives up its last secret. So full is the attention of Tilling's collective consciousness that a very few events satisfy the town's considerable appetite for scandal.

But a sense of claustrophobia is a secondary effect of this economy of allusion. It comes to seem that the number of things available for discussion and even the number of possible developments is absurdly inadequate for human beings endowed with curiosity and ingenuity. One wishes Lucia's problem were different when she confronts in Tilling the same problem of having to speak Italian that she faced at Olga's dinner table in Riseholme not because one is bored with the subject but because it seems too bad that her inventiveness should not be more taxed. Her delicate negotiations with Georgie about their physical relationship are a delight, but they are a reprise of her understanding with Stephen Merriall in *Lucia in London* and foreshadow Mapp's prenuptial agreements with the major. The reader has again a sense of circumscribed possibilities. *Au reservoir,* that poor witticism with which Riseholmites bid each other farewell, is equally endemic in Tilling, suggesting that the world has even a limited number of jokes.

The Tillingites' odd dignity consists in their ability to live in this circumscribed world by treasuring any tidbit or scandal that makes it seem more spacious. Lucia has the camp's gift of transforming her world for others as well as for herself, but, in lesser measure, all of Benson's characters live in imaginary worlds more interesting than their real world—from the Padre, who rejects his drab Manchester origins for a Highland idiom and accent, to Georgie, who fancies himself a boyish rake, to Mapp, whose paranoia enables her to see a cup of tea as witch's brew. The camp imagination celebrates such communal- and self-delusions, knowing that a transformation of the banal into the exotic is frail Life's greatest triumph. What could be more triumphant over all dark energies than Georgie's inspiration to spell out the name of his house with lettering he had commissioned for Lucia's cenotaph—and what could be more *economical* of incident and money in the true Tilling spirit? What could have been more fortuitous than the stonemason's mistake in setting Mapp's name smaller than Lucia's on the memorial stone? Mapp will never forgive the slight, we know, and Tilling will treasure it forever. As a poet once observed, Fortune has its cookies.

The Worshipful Lucia (1935)

A year passes between *Mapp and Lucia* and *The Worshipful Lucia* (published in Britain as *Lucia's Progress*). Lucia finds herself fifty years old at the beginning, slightly bored with her previous successes, and casting about for new projects. Tilling is intensely curious about the abrupt disappearance of Georgie behind closed curtains and about the exact balance of power in the Mapp-Flint marriage, but these mysteries do not engage Lucia deeply. Georgie has shingles, she discovers easily, and the Mapp-Flints clearly wear one trouser leg each. High finance seems a worthy, possibly soul-stirring endeavor, so she establishes herself overnight as a putative expert by following the advice of a London stockbroker named Mammoncash. The Tillingites are soon trying avidly to match her success in the market—so much so that neither gossip, mystery, nor bridge rouse passions equal to that of the *Financial Post,* at least for a time. Lucia makes a great deal of money through her investments, thanks to the unacknowledged Mammoncash; the Mapp-Flints and others do badly.

Other diversions propose themselves to Lucia in due course. When Mapp[9] runs for the borough council on a platform of municipal economy and opposes the clearance of "pretty little slums by the railway," Lucia feels a moral duty to run against her. She is just as high-minded in offering to buy Mallards, ostensibly to give Mapp relief from her losses in the stock market but really because she covets it as the best house in town. No sooner has she taken possession of the house than she fancies there is a hypocaust in the basement and the remains of a Roman temple in the garden. Nothing will do but an archaeological dig. These diversions soon pall, however; the political challenge to Mapp proves an embarrassment when the two women tie for last place in the election, and the archaeological dig proves absurd when its most celebrated treasure is apparently a soft-drink bottle. Success in the stock market enables Lucia to play at municipal philanthropy, however, and to garner an appointed seat on the borough council for the price of some local improvements. Capitalizing on that new distinction, she persuades Georgie to marry her, thus matching Mapp's coup with the major. It is understood by both parties, of course, that there will be no conjugal rights between them. In the last pages, Lucia even anticipates imminent appointment by the borough council as Tilling's mayor.

More so than in other novels of the sequence, real problems lurk in the background of *The Worshipful Lucia,* most notably the problem of sex. It has often been remarked that Benson's characters do not function sexually and, in fact, recoil sharply from physical intimacy. V. S. Pritchett has written appositely on this phenomenon and suggested that Benson's characters are generically neuter. Georgie and Lucia agree enthusiastically never to go to bed together, he says, because they have "that horror" in common. Interestingly, Pritchett links this sexual disinclination to the characters' silence about the Great War, which is a total silence although they live in a post-1918 world lacking in young men and still threatened with rationing.[10] Both these avoidances are fairy-tale fraudulence to Pritchett's way of thinking, but they might also be thought of as camp panache: the one, an audacious ignoring of the war's devastation; the other, a blithe transcendence of the sexual muddle bequeathed by Adam, Queen Victoria, and Freud.

Indeed, Benson's characters suffer too obviously from sexual repression to be considered simply Pritchett's neuters. Homosexual Irene has "an almost embarrassing *schwärmerei*" for Lucia, and she bursts into tears at the news that Lucia and Georgie will marry. Her usual swagger seems an elaborate sexual feint in consequence. Mapp is a figure of fun when she encourages speculation that she is pregnant, since time must be her undoing, but laughter cannot dismiss wholly a whiff of frustrated maternity in the joke. The diminutives that Mapp likes to employ ("sweet little flowers" and the like) seem further evidence of thwarted maternal possibilities, as does her gradual attenuation of "Major Flint" to "Major Benjy" to "Benjy-boy." What is one to make of the preoccupation with incidental pastimes in Tilling except that everyone is as desperate as Mapp to fill nature's void? Of Lucia's ennui, of which the denouement is a marriage of convenience? Can Georgie's passionate attention to his bibelots be understood as anything other than sublimated homosexuality? When Benson does not permit the reader to accompany Georgie and Lucia on their honeymoon, one suspects that his comic imagination quailed before the convolutions of pretense, sublimation, and sexual repression with which he would have had to deal.

Benson's characters are less chary than their creator and refuse to recognize the wages of their sexual repression. Acknowledged inwardly, such repressions tend to fester, as in the dreary literature of neurosis, but turned into social aggression, as in Tilling, they keep the ego humming. When Mapp ends her charade of pregnancy, for instance, a baby cap that she had been knitting for all to see suddenly appears on her own head, much enlarged, "a decoration of artificial campanulas rendering its resemblance to the cap of a hydrocephalous baby less noticeable." It is an audacious gesture, whose spirit one has to admire no matter how ghastly the suggestion that Mapp is her own, misbegotten child. In kindred fashion, the major's sexual unfulfillment seems wholly sublimated in his aggressive golf game, for which he makes no apology. Lucia is so determined that widowhood will not wither her, nor age stale her infinite variety, that she arranges for fifty-one rather than fifty candles on her birthday cake—"to become used to the idea." Even Grosvenor, Lucia's parlormaid, refuses to endure passively the slings and arrows of spinsterhood:

> There were six bells hung close together on a burnished copper frame, and they rang the first six notes of an ascending scale. Grosvenor improvised on these with a small drumstick, and if she was finding life a harmonious business, she often treated Lucia to charming dainty little tunes, quite a pleasure to listen to, though sometimes rather long. Now and then there was an almost lyrical outburst of melody, which caused Lucia a momentary qualm of anxiety lest Grosvenor should have fallen in love and would leave. But if she felt morose or cynical, she expressed her humor with realistic fidelity. Today she struck two adjoining bells very hard, and then ran the drumstick up and down the peal, producing a most jangled effect, which meant that she was jangled, too. "I wonder what's the matter; indigestion perhaps," thought Lucia.

One's continual awareness that such aggressions are psychosexual symptoms makes the camp enterprise of *The Worshipful Lucia* more fragile than in earlier novels but not for that reason less successful. Camp depends upon successes of the spirit rather than of substance, and its victories are most impressive when they transpire on the edge of some human abyss. Lucia understands Grosvenor's code with the bells, for instance, but feels no obligation to offer a sympathetic ear. Instead, she leaves the poor woman "to stew in her own snappishness." That adroit, unfeeling phrase captures exactly her ego's rejection of an involvement that might inhibit its own aggressions. Sympathy can play no significant role in Tilling, obviously, for it would constitute defeat before the psychic aggressions of some other person. Thus it is that people never make a concession in Tilling without demanding some concession for themselves. Diva will not agree to mediate the sale of Mallards unless Mapp agrees to drop the French phrases she has introduced into her speech in imitation of Lucia's Italian. "So confusing," Diva protests, "So ridiculous. All put on." But when Diva in turn has to ask Lucia to give a dinner party that will restore the fractured social life of Tilling, she has to accept a dramaturgy Lucia imposes on the scene. "I?" Lucia queries in her most offensively demure manner. "Little hermit I?" One is told that Diva "could have smacked her for her lofty unconsciousness" but in view of her mission had to check the impulse. Civility is no real help in such negotiations, as Mapp discovers when she interrogates Georgie's cook over the telephone in an attempt to discover the reason for his abrupt seclusion. Indeed, her imitation of Queen Victoria speaking to her Ministers of State proves awkwardly imitable:

> "Could Mrs. Mapp-Flint speak to Mr. Pillson?"
> "No, ma'am, she couldn't. Impossible just now."
> "Is Mrs. Mapp-Flint speaking to Foljambe?"
> "No, ma'am, it's me. Foljambe is out."
> "Mrs. Mapp-Flint will call on Mr. Pillson about four thirty."
> "Very good, ma'am, but I'm afraid Mr. Pillson won't be able to see her."

That the Tillingites do not lose heart despite the frustrations endemic to their repressed sexuality, aggressive egos, and confrontational good manners seems a brave triumph over chaos, achieved from moment to moment. Indeed, they are extraordinary persons despite their obvious failings: buoyant existentialists, characters not at all in search of an author, survivors specie camp. "That's the best of Tilling," says Georgie enthusiastically when Lucia is making one of her vain resolutions to forswear gossip. "There's always something exciting going on. If it isn't one thing it's another, and very often both!"

Trouble for Lucia (1939)

Lucia has been appointed mayor of Tilling in *Trouble for Lucia,* as she had anticipated, and her immediate self-importance in the role exasperates almost everyone. "Egalo-megalo-mayoralo-mania" Georgie terms it as she worries endlessly the question of where he will sit at her inaugural banquet. Her duties as mayor are actually very light, but she makes them as onerous as possible, mulling absurd financial schemes and even a proposal to revive the Elizabethan custom of Tilling supplying fish to the court. When she decides that she must set a mayoral example and no longer play cards for money, she goes too far: Georgie is subsequently invited to play cards without her. Nor is her scheme for a series of municipal lectures a success. Insensitive to the opportunity she affords them to become more widely known, both Desmond McCarthy and Noel Coward decline her invitation to speak.

Indeed, Lucia's genius for manipulating people and events seems to desert her in her official capacity as mayor. She selects Mapp as her mayoress on the theory that the appointment will render her enemy politically harmless, but the appointment stimulates Mapp to greater ambition than before, as Lucia might have anticipated.[11] Mapp's star is thereafter in the ascent. Perfidiously, she opposes Georgie for a seat on the borough council and defeats him with ease. Inexorably, she blocks Lucia from hanging a portrait of herself in the council chambers. Iniquitously, she monopolizes the novelist Susan Legg when she visits the town looking for narrative material that Lucia longs to provide. Irene tries to strike a blow for Lucia with a caricature of Mapp as Botticelli's Venus, but the caricature is so clever that the Royal Academy names it Picture of the Year, and Mapp enjoys a subsequent fame that Lucia envies greatly.

This sad decline of a once-great monarchy reaches its nadir when Lucia makes the mistake of representing a nodding acquaintance with Poppy, the duchess of Sheffield, as a warm friendship. In the strength of her ascendancy, Mapp mocks the exaggeration and persuades Tilling to disbelieve entirely in the relationship, even though Lucia has photographs to certify a memorable half hour she spent with a camera in Poppy's home. It is all very trying; finally, too much to bear. At the conclusion of church services one Sunday morning, hitherto unflappable Lucia vents suddenly her exasperation—"sheer red rage," Benson calls it—and strikes out indiscriminately at the assembled Tillingites. Her stridently solicitous tone is a mockery of their own hypocrisy, a *J'accuse* such as Tilling has never before had to endure:

Dear Susan! No Royce? Have you actually walked all the way from Porpoise Street? You mustn't overdo it! Diva, how is Paddy? He's not been sick again, I hope, after eating one of your delicious sardine tartlets . . .

what a silly mistake I've made; of course, it was the recipe for cream wafers which Susanna's chef gave you which made Paddy so unwell. Irene? You in church? Was it not a lovely sermon, all about thinking evil of your friends? Good morning, Major Benjy. You must get poor Mr. Wyse to try your favorite cure for colds. A tumbler of whiskey, isn't it, every two hours?

Benson then ended the novel on a promissory note, Lucia feeling pleasantly rejuvenated by her cathartic outburst and ready to plot forgiveness. He apparently did not foresee that *Trouble for Lucia* would be the last volume of the sequence—the last novel, in fact, that he would write. Yet it is difficult to imagine what he might further have done with Lucia.[12] As the sequence progresses from innocent Riseholme to iniquitous Tilling and from invincible queenship to barricaded mayorality, it brings Lucia out of a world she dominates too easily into a world that not only offers real opposition to her preposterous queenship but spurns it as an animating principle. The result is a confrontational struggle that brings Lucia closer in each volume to public exposure of her ignorance about music, art, and Italian, and, indeed, any real cultivation of mind and spirit. She has seldom convinced anyone that she *is* cultivated, of course, but the Riseholmites were willing to suspend disbelief because they needed her to galvanize them. In Tilling, her queenship loses prestige daily in a revolutionary atmosphere of *liberté, egalité, rivalité*.

It is symptomatic of Lucia's gradually eroding status in *Trouble for Lucia* that without her advice or encouragement Diva organizes a successful tea shop that becomes the vibrant heart of town life, giving the lie to Mallards' having served that function under either Mapp or Lucia. Increasingly, the townspeople embark on such projects without taking inspiration from Lucia, and they prove capable not only of entrepreneurial successes but of those imaginative embellishments of action, once Lucia's role to inspire, that transform ordinary bad taste into something archly splendid. When Lady Ambermere presents the Riseholme museum with the stuffed remains of a beloved dog, for instance, Lucia takes the situation in hand and returns the macabre gift with a fine show of impudence. But when Susan Wyse takes to wearing as an ornament the cadaver of her late budgerigar, Lucia adds little to the comic developments. She is only the hostess when Blue Birdie falls from

Susan's great bosom into a puddle of raspberry puree and is thereafter indelibly red. When not wearing the cadaver as part of her costume, Susan enshrines it in black onyx and conducts séances in which she communes soulfully with the bird's spirit, thought to be sojourning for the nonce in the Spice Islands. When Mr. Wyse disposes of the grisly remains in fear that Susan is losing her mind, Lucia is helpful in explaining the disappearance as a spiritual dematerialization, but her late entry into the developments is a contrivance, not a true catalyst of the comic action.

Lucia also plays an adumbrated role in the fine saga of Major Benjy's riding crop. The major loses that souvenir of his colonial days when he intends to horsewhip the editor of the *Hampshire Argus* for publishing an unflattering photograph of Mapp. Diverted from that purpose when the editor proffers whiskey, he abandons the crop over a subsequent lunch with the editor in Diva's tearoom, whereupon Diva's dog devours all but the crop's metal cap. Diva buries the cap in her garden to conceal the dog's crime, but Georgie, helping Diva with her tulips, digs it up some months later and turns it over to Lucia. Mapp discovers the cap on Lucia's desk and commissions a replica of the crop—just for devilment—so Lucia commissions a second replica, which is thereupon discovered in the tea shop while the supposed original hangs proudly among the major's collection of Malaysian artifacts. Lucia's mischief embarrasses the Mapp-Flints, of course, but like her explanation about Blue Birdie's disappearance, it is a late element in a sequence of events that courses merrily to disaster without her prodding.

Lucia's commitment to a high-minded mayoralty is largely responsible for her diminished role as a catalyst of events in Tilling. Would Catherine the Great, she asks, have spent her days gambling and gossiping in Diva's tea shop? Her duty, she fancies, is to foster intellectual and artistic activity, social reform, slum clearance, the pasteurization of milk. But of course she cannot entirely quash her delight in surprising Tilling with bourgeois accomplishments, as when she and Georgie learn to ride bicycles, creating a sensation on the High. A doublethink of high- and low-mindedness continues to be her especial audacity—her camp flaunt—however diminished its impact on Tilling's life.

Indeed, the best effects of the novel occur when Lucia's doublethink of high- and low-mindedness brings the worlds of low and high life into conjunction. On the theory that an example is uselessly set if no one follows it, she recants her decision not to gamble and is no sooner welcomed back to Diva's cardroom than her own inspector of police asks for her at the door. Is it a low *raid?* The inspector only wants her official signature on a summons, but Lucia momentarily fears the worst:

> Lucia rose, white to the lips. In a flash there came back to her all her misgivings about the legality of Diva's permitting gambling in a public room, and now the police were raiding it. She pictured headlines in the *Hampshire Argus* and lurid photographs. . . . Raid on Mrs. Godiva Plaistow's gaming rooms. . . . The list of the gamblers caught there. The Mayor and Mayoress of Tilling. . . . A retired Major. The Mayor's husband. The case brought before the Tilling magistrates with the Mayor in the dock instead of on the Bench. Exemplary fines. Her own resignation. Eternal infamy. . . .

Returning a few weeks later with a summons for a female observed speeding recklessly on the mayoral bicycle, the inspector finds a different Lucia, one who confesses promptly to the misdemeanor and demands harsh treatment in her own court. "I will not have one law for the rich and another for the poor in Tilling," she insists superbly, delighted to foster simultaneously a reputation for high-mindedness and for athleticism. Together, the two scenes with the inspector make clear a Lucilic distinction between notoriety and notability and underscore Lucia's ebullient, camp survival in the no-man's-land between them.

One suspects that Benson devised comparatively few such scenes for Lucia in this last novel of the sequence because his unerring instinct for camp wanted to bring Lucia to that climactic moment when all her artifice would be vain. It is a point for which the camp taste yearns, for it is then that artifice can paradoxically snatch failure from almost certain ignominy and create a fragile succès d'estime in a triumph of manner, however wracked, over substance, and in a triumph of illusion over illusion's exposure. As Susan Sontag observes, camp is "the farthest extension, in sensibility, of the metaphor of life as theater."[13] But when Lucia confronts the disbelieving Tillingites after church services at the end of the novel and hurls her anathemas at them like firecrackers, she steps largely, if not entirely, out of the role of the cultivated woman that she has created. That she maintains a semblance of polite phrasing and stagy solicitude is a theatrical victory of sorts, but that she can imagine after such an outburst that forgiveness is hers to bestow is a less public victory, a *succès d'estime de soi même*. It is the sort of victory that can be claimed by Zuleika Dobson and Cardinal Pirelli, too, and it is the only sort of victory that P. G. Wodehouse ever thought of permitting the egregious Bertie Wooster. It is, indeed, the most successful and the most admired performance of camp. Like Zuleika, the cardinal, and Bertie Wooster, Lucia is a stager of her own life who disdains charges of ineptitude by playing insouciantly to herself.

6

Narrative Become Burble: P. G. Wodehouse

Like Benson, P. G. Wodehouse must be numbered among those writers whose prolificacy casts a shadow over their greatness. His bibliographical output has not been determined with exactness, inasmuch as he probably published some early material under unrecognized noms de plume, but under his own name he was the author of nearly a hundred books, ninety-two of them novels and collections of short stories. In addition, he wrote reams of light verse for *Punch,* wrote or collaborated in the writing of sixteen stage productions, and contributed lyrics to twenty-eight musical comedies.[1] A superficial impression of the Wodehouse oeuvre tends to view such prolificacy as evidence of Philistinism—a lack of restraint as quintessentially lowbrow as Wodehouse's view of the idle rich, their butlers, valets, and chefs. Indeed, such an impression of the Wodehouse oeuvre perceives no serious relevance to this world or to any world that has ever existed.

Can a prodigious quantity of such writing command literary attention? In answer to that question, some voices have snorted a great *No!* over the years, but their stimulus has generally been the comic broadcasts that Wodehouse unthinkingly made from Berlin while he was interned in Germany during World War II. In a back-and-forth correspondence in the *Daily Telegraph* that raged for weeks in the wake of his first broadcast, A. A. Milne labeled Wodehouse a political naif; E. C. Bentley (of clerihew fame) protested the honorary degree that Oxford University had awarded Wodehouse years earlier; and Sean O'Casey pronounced him "English Literature's performing flea."[2] The wartime broadcasts were still apparently the issue in 1945 when George Orwell described Wodehouse and his work as fixed forever in the Edwardian age.[3] Wodehouse faced such charges with mildness, as was his way. He volunteered easily in conversation that his degree from Oxford was "bogus" and liked to suggest that he had suffered mental arrest at the age of eighteen.[4] Feigning delight with O'Casey's rude phrase, he even entitled a volume of reminiscences *Performing Flea*.[5]

The truer answer to the question of whether Wodehouse's voluminous writings command literary attention must be affirmative. Just as George Gershwin and Jerome Kern valued Wodehouse as a collaborator and lyricist, so testimonials to his writing abound among those who know the craft of writing. In the 1930s Hilaire Belloc pronounced Wodehouse the best writer of English among his contemporaries,[6] and Auberon Waugh referred to him in 1973 as "the most influential novelist of our age."[7] Dust jackets over the years have reiterated the encomiums of J. B. Priestley ("Mr. Wodehouse is superb") and Compton Mackenzie ("Mr. Wodehouse is beginning to exhaust the superlatives of his critics").[8] An eightieth-birthday salute that proclaimed him "an inimitable international institution and a master humorist" was signed by no less than eighty distinguished writers.[9]

The breadth of Wodehouse's audience suggests that the camp taste cuts through culture both high and low. American shop clerks hoot as readily as Oxbridge academics at the adventures of Psmith, Ukridge, and Bertie Wooster, and they have done so for more than half a century. Different tastes favor different novels of course, but among the great favorites are such masterpieces of camp as *Right Ho, Jeeves, Joy in the Morning, The Mating Season,* and *Bertie Wooster Sees It Through.* All belong to a sequence of novels narrated by a burbling bon vivant named Bertie Wooster and chronicling the misadventures from which his valet Jeeves has to extricate him. The characters have their origin in short stories such as "The Rummy Affair of Old Biffy" that enlivened the pages of the *Saturday Evening Post* in the 1920s. Bertie and Jeeves were soon Wodehouse's most salable commodity, and with the declining market for the short story in the 1930s it was inevitable that the pair should become a mainstay of the Wodehouse novel.[10] Eventually Wodehouse published ten such novels. *Thank You, Jeeves* was the first, followed by *Right Ho, Jeeves, The Code of the Woosters, Joy in the Morning, The Mating Season, Bertie Wooster Sees It Through, Jeeves in the Offing, Stiff Upper Lip, Jeeves, Much Obliged, Jeeves,* and *Aunts Aren't Gentlemen.*

Right Ho, Jeeves (1934)

Right Ho, Jeeves deals with typically Wodehousian confusions. Gussie Fink-Nottle, a fancier of newts, is in love with Madeline Bassett but incapacitated by his shyness from proposing marriage. Like all Bertie's friends, he goes to Jeeves rather than to Bertie for advice. "People are always nettling me like that," observes Bertie, piqued. "Giving me to understand, I mean to say, that in their opinion Bertram Wooster is a mere cipher and that the only member of the household with brains and resources is Jeeves." Jeeves's advice is that Gussie should dress as Mephistopheles for a fancy-dress ball and borrow the confidence from his costume to propose to Madeline. That Gussie fails to arrive at the ball because he has forgotten the address is no fault of Jeeves's plan, but Bertie decides thereupon to superintend the courtship himself. As a first step, he arranges for Gussie to sojourn at Brinkley Court, the Worcestershire home of his Aunt Dahlia, where Madeline is visiting. He argues that the spot is clearly romantic, for he himself has become engaged three times in its rose garden. But confusion, not Cupid, is the genius loci of Brinkley Court. Aunt Dahlia has lost at baccarat money that her husband gave her to pay the bills of *Milady's Boudoir,* a magazine she publishes, and she is afraid he will divorce her if she asks for more money. Her daughter Angela (Bertie's cousin) has broken her engagement to Tuppy Glossop and is both distraught and angry. Most alarming to Bertie, Aunt Dahlia has arranged for him to make a speech at a prize-giving ceremony at Market Snodsbury Grammar School.

Determined to prove himself more adept than Jeeves at solving such problems, Bertie devises a solution for Gussie's problem that seems to him eminently adaptable to Aunt Dahlia's and Tuppy's problems as well. His solution is that all should profess no appetite for the meals prepared by Anatole, Aunt Dahlia's excellent French chef, thereby inviting solicitous inquiry from the appropriate parties. His solution to the Market Snodsbury problem is that Gussie will speak in his stead, thereby impressing Madeline. The sudden abstinence at table is noticed only by Anatole, of course, and his immediate resignation shakes the foundation of well-being at Brinkley Court. Gussie's well-oiled performance at Market Snodsbury is equally disastrous—possibly the best scene of its kind in the annals of farce. Adding to the confusion, Madeline Bassett decides Bertie is in love with her, as is her habit in the novels whenever her current fiancé proves suddenly unworthy. "The exquisite code of politeness of the Woosters prevented me clipping her one on the ear-hole," Bertie confides to the reader, "but I would have given a shilling to be able to do it. There seemed to me something deliberately fatheaded in the way she persisted in missing the gist." The confusion escalates: soon Angela is halfheartedly engaged to Gussie; Bertie, to Madeline.

Asked once again for advice, Jeeves suggests that Bertie set off a midnight fire alarm in the course of which Tuppy will be inspired to rescue Angela, and Gussie, Madeline. Bertie implements the plan, but the aggrieved lovers fail to throw themselves into the right arms, and the household finds itself locked out of the house in the wee hours. Jeeves quickly arranges that Bertie should bicycle eighteen miles to a servants' ball for a spare key, thought to be in the butler's pocket. Actually, Jeeves has possessed himself of the spare key in advance and engineered events so that the assorted couples will be united in exasperation with Bertie, fall into the proper arms, and forgive even Bertie in the general delight that he is bicycling unhappily about the countryside. Although sore in the leg muscles, Bertie must concede in the last pages that Jeeves has succeeded where he had failed.

This summary of the novel's plot does not adequately suggest the clockwork precision with which Wodehouse provides motivations for every exit and entrance of a character, keeps straight the tangle of misunderstandings and cross-purposed conversations, and orchestrates the interactions of the several lines of development. He worried enormously about such intricacies, considering them much the harder part of writing, yet considered that there was insufficient plotting in his novels as a rule. "I was conscious all the time that the plot was not too strong," he wrote to his agent in 1934 with regard to *Right Ho, Jeeves,* "so I developed every possible chance there was for bright dialogue."[11] Bertie Wooster complains ritualistically about the difficulties of organizing his narrative at the beginning of *Right Ho, Jeeves,* as at the beginning of other narratives, at once representing and parodying Wodehouse's own concern:

> I don't know if you have had the same experience, but the snag I always come up against when I'm telling a story is this dashed difficult problem of where to begin it. It's a thing you don't want to go wrong over, because one false step and you're sunk. I mean, if you fool about too long at

the start, trying to establish atmosphere, as they call it, and all that sort of rot, you fail to grip and the customers walk out on you.

Get off the mark, on the other hand, like a scalded cat, and your public is at a loss. It simply raises its eyebrows, and can't make out what you're talking about.

And in opening my report of the complex case of Gussie Fink-Nottle, Madeline Bassett, my Cousin Angela, my Aunt Dahlia, my Uncle Thomas, young Tuppy Glossop and the cook, Anatole, with the above spot of dialogue, I see that I have made the second of these two floaters.

One cannot escape an impression that the three-act economy of musical comedy shaped Wodehouse's sense of narrative development. The resolutely blithe and yet finically tidy plot of *Right Ho, Jeeves* is a brilliant throwaway—excessively patterned in the tradition of musical comedy plots so that the audience suffers no suspense or questions that might distract them from the moment-to-moment glitter of presentation. The audience knows Bertie will botch his attempts to manipulate the lovers as surely as it knows the lovers will be united satisfactorily by Jeeves because that is the tradition of such weightlessly rigorous plotting. As Robert Hall has pointed out, the influence of musical comedy is further evident in the tendency of Wodehouse's characters to correspond to stock types of the musical stage: juvenile leads, major comic characters, bit parts, and so forth.[12] Such plotting is also in the spirit of classic commedia dell'arte, in which formulaic plotting permitted flourishes of improvisation that were the real entertainment. One could do worse than to understand Aunt Dahlia as Pantaloon redivivus, Jeeves as Arlecchino, Bertie as Punch.

The improvisations that such stock plotting throw into relief in Wodehouse's novel are primarily linguistic. An exchange of telegrams between Aunt Dahlia and Bertie serves in a small way to advance the plot, but it is more substantially an occasion for stylistic play. Bertie's telegrams are stubbornly uncomprehending; Dahlia's, sophomorically withering; yet both sets are affectionately tagged. As the exchange goes on, parsimonious Dahlia becomes as contemptuous of telegraphic economy as of the eyes of clerks who may be scandalized by the exchange. The ripeness of expression is all:

—*Come at once. Travers.*
—*Perplexed. Explain. Bertie.*
—*What on earth is there to be perplexed about, ass? Come at once. Travers.*

—*How do you mean come at once? Regards. Bertie.*
—*I mean come at once, you maddening half-wit. What did you think I meant? Come at once or expect an aunt's curse first post tomorrow. Love. Travers.*
—*When you say "When you say Come" do you mean "Come to Brinkley Court"? And when you say "At once" do you mean "at once"? Fogged. At a loss. All the best. Bertie.*
—*Yes, yes, yes, yes, yes, yes, yes. It doesn't matter whether you understand or not. You just come at once, as I tell you, and for heaven's sake stop this backchat. Do you think I am made of money that I can afford to send you telegrams every ten minutes. Stop being a fathead and come immediately. Love. Travers.*

Similarly, Dahlia's confrontation with Bertie after the midnight fire alarm is not so much a development of the plot as it is the occasion for a stylistic flourish. Her careful banalities and mock solicitude threaten that she will have Bertie incarcerated in a mental asylum, but the threat is obviously pro forma. Intellectually and emotionally disengaged from the possibility, the reader is free to enjoy the counterpoint of her extravagantly ominous politeness and Bertie's guarded admissions:

"Well, Bertie dear," she said, "here we all are."
"Quite," I replied guardedly.
"Nobody missing, is there?"
"I don't think so."
"Splendid. So much healthier for us out in the open like this than frowsting in bed. I had just dropped off when you did your bell-ringing act. For it was you, my sweet child, who rang that bell, was it not?"
"I did ring the bell, yes."
"Any particular reason, or just a whim? . . . Tell Aunt Dahlia."

The stylistic interplay between Bertie and Jeeves is similar to that between aunt and nephew. On the one hand Jeeves is unflappable, pedantically precise and allusive, inexpressive except for a right eyebrow that is occasionally permitted to twitch. Donaldson calls him "a man with a dictionary of quotations where his heart ought to be."[13] On the other hand, Bertie is impulsive, breezily unintellectual, amiably inexact in statement and quotation—"an endearing ass" according to Usborne.[14] Not wanting to believe Jeeves's report that Gussie had called for him, Bertie says, "The chap I know wears horn-rimmed spectacles and has a face like a fish. How does that check up with your data?" Jeeves responds with a linguistic snub: "The gentleman who came to the flat wore horn-rimmed spectacles, sir." The tension escalates as Bertie demands his pound of fish: "And looked like something on a slab?" But Jeeves will not be routed into indecorum: "Possibly there was a certain suggestion of the piscine, sir." On another occasion, Jeeves observes that "aberrations of memory are not uncommon with those who, like Mr. Fink-Nottle, belong essentially to what one might call the dreamer type." "One might also call it the fatheaded type," Bertie shoots back. His impulse is not really to translate what Jeeves has said but to challenge the mode of its saying. It is a game between master and servant never admitted between them (or to the reader), but consciously played.

The improvisations of this stylistic gamesmanship resolutely upstage developments in the plot. Gussie Fink-Nottle burbling uncontrollably about newts at a crucial moment in romancing Madeline Bassett is a case in point—an event so predictable and essentially trite that Wodehouse does not trouble to show it. Recounted to Bertie in Jeeves's fussy and pedantic style, however, the event is handsomely ludicrous:

> Mr. Fink-Nottle was the victim of a sudden unfortunate spasm of nervousness, sir. Upon finding himself alone with the young lady, he admits to having lost his morale. In such circumstances, gentlemen frequently talk at random, saying the first thing that chances to enter their heads. This, in Mr. Fink-Nottle's case, would seem to have been the newt, its treatment in sickness and in health.

And from a stylistic viewpoint, the event is still richer for Bertie's translating it into his own prattle:

> The scales fell from my eyes. I understood. I had had the same sort of thing happen to me in moments of crisis. I remember once detaining a dentist with the drill at one of my lower bicuspids and holding him up for nearly ten minutes with a story about a Scotchman, an Irishman, and a Jew. Purely automatic. The more he tried to jab, the more I said "Hoots, mon," "Begorrah," and "Oy, oy."

This continual joggling of linguistic styles one against another expresses a generally comic relationship in the novel between elemental human nature and the alleged refinements of the allegedly cultivated upper class. It is Wodehouse's basic joke that the upper class has less refinement of manner than its servants; the original twist he gives the joke is that only servants pretend otherwise. Characters like Bertie and Aunt Dahlia stand occasionally on their rank, to be sure, but they are more often than not indifferent to standards of cultivation and entirely willing to run amok through the proprieties. It is a willingness baroquely convoluted on occasion, as when Bertie congratulates himself on *not* telling Gussie that he is "an offence to the eyesight." Dahlia cares nothing for even such minimal self-restraint and is capable of greeting Bertie with a heartfelt "Hullo, eyesore." If such remarks have a sociological background—reducible on Bertie's part to public-school badinage, and on Dahlia's to habits of expression acquired on the hunting field—they are just sufficiently so to keep the reader morally off-balance.

Morality is never really a factor in the Wodehouse world, of course. The crudity of the upper classes in both speech and feeling is only temperamental extravagance, an eruptive venting of spleen in which malice plays no role. "Tut," Bertie says good-humoredly to Aunt Dahlia on an occasion when she attacks his character, but she is in no mood for even such a mild rebuke:

> "What did you say?"
> "I said, 'Tut!'"
> "Say it once again, and I'll biff you where you stand. I've enough to endure without being tutted at."
> "Quite."
> "Any tutting that's required, I'll attend to myself. And the same applies to clicking the tongue, if you were thinking of doing that."

When he senses that Jeeves disapproves of something he means to do, Bertie is as capable as Aunt Dahlia of putting down mutiny in the ranks, but his class arrogance loses its edge on the granite imperturbability of Jeeves as surely as Aunt Dahlia's is worn down by his own, resolute obtuseness. All such rebukes are inspirations of the moment—stylistic jeux d'esprit meant less to affect events than momentarily to palliate the speaker:

> "Jeeves," I said, "Don't keep saying 'Indeed, sir?' No doubt nothing is further from your mind than to convey such a suggestion, but you have a way of stressing the 'in' and then coming down with a thud on

the 'deed' which makes it virtually tantamount to 'Oh, yeah?' Correct this, Jeeves."

Again,

"I don't want to seem always to be criticizing your methods of voice production, Jeeves," I said, "but I must inform you that that 'Well, sir' of yours is in many respects fully as unpleasant as your 'Indeed, sir?' Like the latter, it seems to be tinged with a definite skepticism. It suggests a lack of faith in my vision. The impression I retain after hearing you shoot it at me a couple of times is that you consider me to be talking through the back of my neck, and that only a feudal sense of what is fitting restrains you from substituting for it the words 'Says you!'"

Stylistic gaucherie such as "biff you where you stand," "Oh, yeah?" and "Says you!" are the ineffable charm of *Right Ho, Jeeves,* as of all novels in the series. No one is better than Wodehouse at concocting that distinctive stew of half-remembered quotations, circumlocutions, aggressively voguish slang, and preposterous analogies that constitute the burble of his best characters. A heartlessness indistinguishable from naiveté spices the mix. Bertie informs us that Angela was very nearly "inhaled" by a shark while aquaplaning in the sea off Cannes, at which point she felt "like a salted almond at a public dinner." Callously, he alludes to Gussie's beloved newts as "dumb chums." "Tup, Tushy!" he says dismissively to the heartbroken Glossop—"I mean, Tush, Tuppy!"

The waywardness of such burble is due largely to linguistic influences that Bertie regurgitates with no regard for context. Jeeves is his primary source of fractured and misapplied quotations. With no apparent intention to be flippant, Bertie says of Glossop, "The man seemed sandbagged. Melancholy, as I remember Jeeves saying once about Pongo Twistleton when he was trying to knock off smoking, had marked him for her own." A fondness for thrillers has left Bertie with his inexhaustible store of cliché, much of it empurpled. After abandoning Gussie to a plate of sandwiches in Aunt Dahlia's rose garden, he observes, "Presently from behind us there sounded in the night the splintering crash of a well-kicked plate of ham sandwiches, accompanied by the muffled oaths of a strong man in his wrath." Indeed, Bertie is a stylistic magpie, his effects apt to be drawn from anywhere. His fondness for the racetrack shapes the narrative engagingly when he describes how he, Aunt Dahlia, and her butler Seppings rushed to Anatole's room to dissuade Gussie from making faces through a skylight at that sensitive chef:

> I had always known her as a woman who was quite active on her pins, but I had never suspected her of being capable of the magnificent burst of speed which she now showed. Pausing merely to get a rich hunting-field expletive off her chest, she was out of the room and making for the stairs before I could swallow a sliver of—I think—banana. And feeling, as I had felt when I got that telegram of hers about Angela and Tuppy, that my place was by her side, I put down my plate and hastened after her, Seppings following at a loping gallop.
>
> I say that my place was by her side, but it was not so dashed easy to get there, for she was setting a cracking pace. At the top of the first flight she must have led by a matter of half a dozen lengths, and was still shaking off my challenge when she rounded into the second. At the next landing, however, the gruelling going appeared to tell on her, for she slackened off a trifle and showed symptoms of roaring, and by the time we were in the straight we were running practically neck and neck. Our entry into Anatole's room was as close a finish as you could have wished to see.
>
> Result:
>
> 1. *Aunt Dahlia.*
> 2. *Bertram.*
> 3. *Seppings.*
>
> *Won by short head. Half a staircase separated second and third.*

The effect is vintage Bertram and entirely camp: the irreverent "pins"; the enthusiast's "magnificent" to describe Aunt Dahlia's speed; the fastidiously expurgated "hunting-field expletive"; the distractedly precise "a sliver of—I think—banana"; the platitudinous "my place was at her side"; these, and a dozen other happily infelicitous phrases; above all, the horse-race analogy, ludicrously and self-indulgently sustained while the domestic harmony of Brinkley Court lies in peril. Of such effects Wodehouse is a master.

Joy in the Morning (1946)

The events of *Joy in the Morning* are set in motion by Lord Percival Worplesdon, the second husband of Bertie Wooster's Aunt Agatha—that *other* aunt whom Bertie often describes as eating broken bottles for breakfast, wearing barbed wire next to her skin, and conducting human sacrifice by moonlight. About to conclude a shipping agreement with the American magnate J. Chichester Clam, Worplesdon asks Jeeves's advice on how to meet with Clam in secret so as to avoid a run on the market.[15] Jeeves suggests that Bertie occupy Wee Nookie, a cottage on the Worplesdon estate at Steeple Bumpleigh, and make the cottage available for clandestine meetings. The plan falls in with Jeeves's desire to get in some fishing on the estate, but it does not fall in at all with Bertie's resolution to stay far away from Steeple Bumpleigh. Scarcely less palatable to him than Aunt Agatha are Worplesdon's two children by a first marriage: Lady Florence Craye, an "aunt-in-training" to whom he was once accidentally engaged, and Edwin the Boy Scout, ferret-faced and pestiferous with good deeds. It does not enhance the charm of Steeple Bumpleigh that the local constable is G. D'Arcy ("Stilton") Cheesewright, a muscular and muscle-headed classmate of Bertie's who is newly engaged to Florence Craye. The presence in the village of Boko Fittleworth, a friend engaged to Nobby Hopwood (a ward of Lord Worplesdon), does not tempt Bertie to leave the relative safety of London. "I don't know if you have ever seen one of those old maps where they mark a spot with a cross and put 'Here be dragons' or 'Keep ye eye skinned for Hippogriffs,'" he remarks, "but I had always felt that some such kindly warning might well have been given to pedestrians and traffic with regard to this Steeple Bumpleigh."

Several considerations reconcile Bertie to taking up residence in Wee Nookie nonetheless. He discovers in himself an instinct to save Stilton from a woman who obviously wants to improve his mind; he is persuaded that compliance with Jeeves's plan will give him the right to ask Lord Worplesdon to withdraw his opposition to Nobby marrying Boko; and he is cravenly fearful of incurring Aunt Agatha's displeasure. Steeple Bumpleigh proves instantly inhospitable, of course. Thinking him Edwin, Boko hurls a figurine at Bertie in greeting, and jealous Stilton accuses him immediately of "snake in the grassing" with Florence. When Edwin burns Wee Nookie to the ground in an effort to welcome Bertie with a good deed, Lord Worplesdon charges Bertie with arson and threatens to commit him to an asylum for the criminally deranged. "The curse has come upon me," moans Bertie to Jeeves.

Bertie is indeed cursed in *Joy in the Morning*, for he is largely innocent of plotting and simply caught up in the machinations of others. He does not know when he agrees to plead the cause of Boko's engagement to Nobby that Boko had tried to amuse Lord Worplesdon with trick novelties like The Plate Lifter, The Dribble Glass, and The Surprise Salt Shaker. It is Boko's idea, not Bertie's, to stage a fake burglary the day Worplesdon's theft insurance expires and then to lock the claustrophobic J. Chichester Clam in a potting shed under the assumption that he has apprehended a real burglar. It is Florence who breaks with Stilton over his insistence that Boko be arrested for his part in the potting-shed debacle, and it is she who resuscitates a nonexistent proposal of marriage from Bertie. And it is Jeeves who decides to steal Stilton's uniform for Bertie to wear at a masked ball, infuriating that dimwitted constable against his putative rival in love.

Jeeves finally orchestrates general forgiveness and appropriate happy endings. Under threat of Aunt Agatha's being informed that he has attended a masked ball in her absence, Lord Worplesdon gives Boko and Nobby his blessing. Stilton is at the same time reaffianced to Florence, having withdrawn his insistence that Boko and Bertie be arrested. Bertie and Jeeves thereupon take their leave before further explanations become necessary, before Florence Craye can imperil Bertie's bachelorhood once again, and before the dread Aunt Agatha can return. It occurs to Bertie that biographers will probably allude to this period of his life as "The Steeple Bumpleigh Horror."

Joy in the Morning is generally regarded as one of the best Wodehouse novels.[16] Among the great pleasures of the novel is the interaction of its farcical developments with an economy of presentation more suggestive of the well-made play than of farce. Bertie picks up a book in a shop, for instance, finds himself holding a romantic novel by Florence Craye, and discovers the author herself unexpectedly on the scene, misty-eyed with a gratitude that threatens to revive their former betrothal. His stumbling upon the book is as opportunely theatrical a contrivance as a glove or letter discovered in a first act, and the effect is delicately camp. Farce is not inconsistent with such a theatrically derivative economy, of course, but farce counterpoises its clockwork of events with a suppleness of life entirely missing in the world of Bertie and Jeeves.[17] Indeed, that Bertie hurries subsequently to a jewelry shop and meets Stilton buying an engagement ring for Florence renders the sequence of his shopping errands so contrived an exposition of circumstances that it seems a send-up of all artistic economies.

An effervescent mix of calculation and miscalculation is another camp pleasure that Wodehouse affords the reader of *Joy in the Morning*. Reminding Bertie that Florence had broken her engagement to Boko when he booted Edwin in the seat of his pants, Jeeves points out that Master Edwin is just then stooping over some object on the ground that has engaged his attention. "There is a tide in the affairs of men which, taken at the flood, leads on to fortune," he expostulates richly. "Omitted, all the voyage of their life is bound in shallows and in miseries." He immediately summons Lady Florence to witness the spectacle that shall cause her to break her second engagement to Bertie. But a superb kick by which Bertie sends Edwin "travelling as if out of a gun" inspires Florence to an "Ah!" practically indistinguishable from *Whoopee!* In a twist of the plot, she herself has fallen victim to a good deed, and her gratitude to Bertie for booting Edwin cements their betrothal.

If Florence's off-again/on-again engagement to Bertie recalls that of the predacious Madeline Bassett in *Right Ho, Jeeves,* the economy is typically Wodehousian. Bertie's adventures with butlers, aunts, and policemen reprise themselves in the novels, too, just as the novels begin routinely with Bertie denying Jeeves some small concession and end with the concession made in gratitude for Jeeves's intervention in a crisis. Indeed, events and circumstances duplicate themselves to such an extent that Bertie's world comes to seem rigidly formulaic. Girls who break their engagements always announce themselves affianced to Bertie; stuffy uncles are always former rakes, cowed into domesticity by their wives; and with the exception of Aunt Dahlia, aunts are invariably throwbacks to the Mesozoic era. (The sound of "Aunt calling to Aunt like mastodons bellowing across primeval swamps" is to Bertie the most terrifying sound in nature and one of the most familiar.) Small boys are always fiends incarnate in the Wodehouse world; small dogs are always ferocious biters of ankles; and babies are always ugly. Handsome men are axiomatically dim-witted, and literary women, it can be assumed, will try to improve a fellow's mind. Bedrooms are equally useful for crowd scenes and for concealing people in cupboards but never useful for slumber because someone will have short-sheeted the bed or punctured the hot water bottle—in which case the mantelpiece will contain a china figure of the Infant Samuel at Prayer that is useful to be thrown to the floor in exasperation. Policemen are meant to be separated from their helmets and sometimes from their complete uniforms—to be left in a state of nature, as it were, by a law of nature. In short, life in the Wodehouse world recycles endlessly a very limited number of situations and experiences. The Pandora's Box that each novel opens anew has the limited repertoire of a jack-in-the-box.

This circumscription of the Wodehouse world permits Bertie and the other characters to be unusually candid. They can say the most appalling things about one another because they risk little in a world that foreordains both chaos and its resolutions. In effect, they live in the world of animated cartoons, wherein a character flattened by a steamroller inflates blithely into shape again. The most fundamental pleasure of such a world is that it affords the audience a holiday from conscience. There is something morally liberating about Nobby's pronouncing Boko "a miserable fathead" with no real thought for his feelings; about Florence's fulminating that Stilton is "an obstinate, mulish, pigheaded, overbearing, unimaginative, tyrannical jack in office"; about Boko's alluding to Florence as a "black spot" he had thought he passed into Stilton's possession. It adds to the fun that Bertie thinks women alone vent such spleen—"just for the fun of the thing and to keep the pores open." "You can't go by what a girl says, when she's giving you the devil for making a chump of yourself," he instructs Boko. "It's like Shakespeare. Sounds well, but doesn't mean anything." The blood lust that women sometimes betray in speech is a fact of life in his chauvinistic view, simply an atavistic urge. "Love's silken bonds are not broken," he suggests, "just because the female half of the sketch takes umbrage at the looney behaviour of the male partner and slips it across him in a series of impassioned speeches. However devoutly a girl may worship the man of her choice, there always comes a time when she feels an irresistible urge to haul off and let him have it in the neck."

In the innocence of their circumscribed world, Wodehouse's characters are free to indulge even darkly sadistic fantasies. Having inadvertently been locked by Boko in a garage, Lord Worplesdon thinks of skinning his jailor alive, "lingeringly and with a blunt knife." Bertie says memorably of Edwin, "There's a boy who makes you feel that what this country wants is somebody like King Herod." The most casual expressions of the characters hint at disproportionate violence, as in Bertie's reiterated statement that someone taken by surprise has been "struck in the small of the back by the Cornish Express." Irritating remarks prompt fantasies of inordinate retribution, as when a foolish statement by Nobby persuades Bertie that her entire sex should be suppressed. The animal world is not exempt from such richly imagined violence. Hedgehogs concealed between bedsheets turn instantly into "fretful porpentines"; Boko's customary dishevelment suggests that of "a parrot . . . dragged through a hedge backwards." In the moral anarchy of the novel, Bertie claims the status of religious experience for the few moments of actual violence. Learning that Edwin has cracked Lord Worplesdon on the head with a hockey stick, he attests to "that sort of awed feeling one gets sometimes, when one has a close-up of the workings of Providence and realizes that nothing is put into this world without a purpose, not even Edwin, and that the meanest creatures have their uses."

It is important to the amoral good fun of *Joy in the Morning* that this taste for violence is almost entirely verbal. Physical violence is limited to bashing the heads of assumed burglars, kicking Boy Scouts in the seats of their trousers, and fending off killer-Pekingese. And if the characters deal in psychological violence by saying terrible things to one another, it is significant that the victims of verbal aggression do not generally protest their bad usage. Upon his arrival in Steeple Bumpleigh, Bertie greets Boko with a typically offensive speech: "I was saying to Nobby, whom I drove down here in my car, how extraordinary it was that any girl should have fallen in love with you at first sight. I wouldn't have thought it could be done." Boko's lack of umbrage is also typical. "It came as quite a surprise to me, too," he agrees. "I don't wonder," Bertie responds—as if the polite, dispassionate exchange might continue forever. On another occasion, with no thought for the casual offensiveness of his terms, Bertie evokes a sudden recognition of Stilton: "That beefy frame. . . That pumpkin-shaped head. . . The face that looked like a slab of pink dough. . . It was none other than my old friend, Stilton Cheesewright." That Stilton shows no enthusiasm for their meeting might seem an intuitive response on his part to the insulting terms of Bertie's recognition, but Wodehouse demands of the reader a more complex understanding, for Bertie endures unprotestingly a widespread distaste for his person not to be compared with the physiological distaste he expresses for Stilton:

At a moment like this, with old boyhood friends meeting again after long separation, I mean to say, you might have expected a good deal of animated what-ho-ing and an immediate picking up of the threads. Of this, however, there was a marked absence. The Auld Lang Syne spirit was strong in me, but not, or I was mistaken, equally strong in G. D'Arcy Cheesewright. *I have met so many people in my time who have wished that Bertram was elsewhere that I have come to recognize the signs.* [emphasis mine]

The ease and frequency with which Bertie observes that people wish him elsewhere suggests that he is virtually without conventional egotism. He fancies he has good judgment in matters sartorial and is forever claiming endowments of a specifically Wooster sort ("We Woosters can read between the lines," "It is seldom that the Woosters think only of self"), but these sources of pride are so entirely groundless as to seem innocent affectations. The truer measure of Bertie's egotism is the casual admission that he is generally despised, so often repeated that it lends his character a touching innocence. Wanting to ingratiate Boko with her father, Florence suggests that Bertie say Boko saved his life as a boy, but knowing his poor standing with Lord Worplesdon, Bertie argues that her father would be more favorably impressed had Boko turned his boyhood energies to assassination. Conscious on another occasion that Cheesewright wants to be rid of him, Bertie is instantly indignant—but not from any conventional impulse of egotism:

I looked at him, amazed. Did he really imagine, I asked myself, that I was as easily got rid of as this? Why, experts have tried to get rid of Bertram Wooster and have been forced to admit defeat.

This innocence of Bertie Wooster is the special appeal of *Joy in the Morning,* even the key to its success. Were the novel more purely farcical, Bertie would be a rogue who escapes a deserved fate as he careens through various affairs of the heart and almost all the proprieties of language. But Bertie in no way deserves either marriage to Florence, incarceration in Stilton's jail, or the unimaginable torments Aunt Agatha might devise for him. One must be impressed that comedy does not ordinarily dare to afflict the truly innocent man with so much inconvenience as Bertie endures. It is the camp artistry of *Joy in the Morning* and the source of its amoral fun that Bertie is indeed guilty of terrible offenses—but against proprieties operative in the reader's world, not in his own—and that he is at the same time innocent of indiscretions that the reader applauds when others commit them in Bertie's name. Few novels in the English tradition have dismissed the world of conventional morality so blithely.

The Mating Season (1949)

As its title suggests, *The Mating Season* is about young love in its season—or, to be more precise, in the village of King's Deverill, to which Bertie has been ordered by Aunt Agatha so that he might lend his services to an entertainment sponsored by friends of hers, the sisters Charlotte, Emmeline, Harriet, and Myrtle Deverill and Dame Daphne Winkworth. The ladies are the collective aunts of rich and handsome Esmond Haddock, and they disapprove greatly of his amorous involvement with Corky Pirbright, a Hollywood starlet who is organizing the entertainment. They disapprove equally of the engagement of their respective niece and daughter, Gertrude Winkworth, to Corky's brother "Catsmeat," a Hollywood actor who is Bertie's good friend. Dame Daphne is godmother to Madeline Bassett, and the aunts are eager to meet her fiancé, the newt-loving Gussie Fink-Nottle, so that they might disapprove of him, too. Indeed, Gussie is scheduled to visit the aunts at Deverill Hall sans Madeline at the same time as Bertie.

The situation becomes tricky when Gussie is sentenced to fourteen days in jail for wading in the Trafalgar Square fountain in pursuit of newts, for if Madeline should discover Gussie's bad judgment she is apt to reaffiance herself to Bertie, whose code of honor will not permit him to deny the engagement. So Bertie goes to Deverill Hall saying he *is* Gussie. Gussie's sentence is subsequently remitted, and he arrives at the Hall claiming—what else?—to be Bertie. In short order, Catsmeat pretends to be "Meadowes," a valet to Bertie in his role as Gussie, and Jeeves attends the real Gussie in his role as Bertie in order to conceal the truth from the butler, who happens to be Jeeves's uncle. The confusions of role and relationship at Deverill Hall are not lessened when Gussie develops a crush on Corky, when Esmond Haddock pretends to be in love with Gertrude in order to make Corky jealous, and when Queenie the parlormaid announces herself betrothed to Catsmeat upon their being discovered in a vaguely compromising tête-à-tête.

Preparations for the entertainment proceed amid whirligig complications. Bertie was originally engaged to perform a cross-talk routine with a local constable named Dobbs, but Dobbs becomes anathema to Corky when he plagues the local minister (her uncle) with atheistic remarks about Jonah and the Whale. The relationship between Corky and Dobbs is not improved when her enormous dog, Sam Goldwyn, is incarcerated for biting the constable. Gussie thereupon arranges a plague of frogs for the constable and a jail-break for Sam Goldwyn, in pursuit of whom Dobbs literally *trees* Gussie. Jeeves coshes the constable from behind as he stands beneath the tree, and Dobbs experiences the coshing as a thunderbolt from heaven, à la Saul of Tarsus. An immediate resurgence of religious faith permits his betrothal to Queenie, who had objected until that time to his low atheism. In a subsequent chain of events, carefully plotted by Jeeves, Esmond's performance in the entertainment is a great success because Jeeves has stocked the audience with paid enthusiasts; success then gives Esmond the courage to defy his aunts in support of Gertrude when she throws herself into Catsmeat's arms; and Esmond's courage vis-a-vis the aunts inspires Corky to accept his long-standing proposal of marriage. Gussie's affections revert at the same time to Madeline Bassett, who promises him a life less filled with incident than life with Corky. The array of sundered and reunited hearts in King's Deverill comes out exactly in balance, Bertie reports happily. "If there is one thing that is the dish of the decent-minded man," he observes, "it is seeing misunderstandings between loving hearts cleared up, especially in the springtime."

As Richard Usborne has pointed out, *The Mating Season* offers evidence that Wodehouse had not entirely forgiven those persons who judged harshly his wartime broadcasts from Berlin.[18] In a moment of inspiration, Gussie gives his name as Alfred Duff Cooper when brought to justice after the Trafalgar Square incident, and he commemorates thereby Duff Cooper, who was the minister of information that sponsored William "Cassandra" Connor's attack on Wodehouse over the airwaves of the BBC. Miss Eustacia Pulbrook is an inept violinist in the King's Deverill entertainment and an obvious allusion to Sir Eustace Pulbrook, who denounced Wodehouse although they were both old boys of Dulwich College. That the Winnie-the-Pooh verses Bertie is condemned to recite at the entertainment seem to him cause for audience resentment could not have pleased A. A. Milne, who had written a patronizing letter about his old friend to the *Daily Telegraph*. But such allusions are incidental in a text resolutely comic and not significantly vengeful. Wodehouse had some regrets about his years working for MGM in Hollywood, too, but the purest affection colors his portraits of Hollywood film stars like Corky and Catsmeat—his portrait, especially, of Mrs. Clara Wellbeloved, an infirm old lady devoted to Hollywood lore. Corky visits her in an effort to help her uncle with his parish duties and reports to Bertie that

> she knows exactly how many times everybody's been divorced and why, how much every picture for the last twenty years has grossed, and how many Warner brothers there are. She even knows how many times Artie Shaw has been married, which I'll bet he couldn't tell you himself. She asked if I had ever married Artie Shaw, and when I said No, seemed to think I was pulling her leg or must have done it without noticing. I tried to explain that when a girl goes to Hollywood she doesn't *have* to marry Artie Shaw, it's optional, but I don't think I convinced her.

If the reader senses Wodehouse's own experience of filmland and its devotees informing such a passage, it is because the author enjoys flirting with auctorial self-disclosure in a camp manner. Bertie Wooster's ineptitude as a narrator is actually a mock ineptitude that plays against Wodehouse's skill and permits an interplay between formal notions of story telling and a cavalier implementation of those notions by author and narrator simultaneously:

> But half a jiffy. I'm forgetting that you haven't the foggiest what all this is about. It so often pans out that way when you begin a story. You whizz off the mark all pep and ginger, like a mettlesome charger going into its routine, and the next thing you know, the customers are up on their hind legs, yelling for footnotes.

Again,

> In dishing up this narrative for family consumption, it has been my constant aim throughout to get the right word in the right place and to avoid fobbing the customers off with something weak and inexpressive when they have a right to expect the telling phrase. It means a bit of extra work, but one has one's code.

The author and narrator evoke each other in the same way when Bertie submits for Gussie's approval a Pat-and-Mike routine that Catsmeat has written. Wodehouse's long experience in the theater clearly informs the passage, the more wittily for the flourish of Bertie's theatrical innocence:

> He took the script and studied it with a sullen frown. Watching him, I realized what a ghastly job it must be writing plays. I mean, having to hand over your little effort to a hardfaced manager and stand shuffling your feet while he glares at it as if it hurt him in a tender spot, preparatory to pushing it back at you with a curt "It stinks."

In a similar manner, Wodehouse's well-publicized fondness for dogs enriches the inevitable moment in every novel of the series when Bertie must deal with a hostile Pekingese or a large, overly friendly dog like Sam Goldwyn. His biographer points out that "all his life [Wodehouse] would lavish on animals the stores of affection he could not bestow on man" and that he had "an obsessive love of pekes."[19] It is a camp inversion of that love that Bertie *loathes* Pekingese and views affectionate dogs the way Wodehouse viewed his human familiars—as overly intimate in dispositional tendency. Jeeves is even more of a mock rebuke than Bertie to Wodehouse's weakness for canine inamoratos:

> What ensued was rather like the big scene in *The Hound of the Baskervilles.* The baying and the patter of feet grew louder, and suddenly out of the darkness Sam Goldwyn clocked in, coming along at a high rate of speed and showing plainly in his manner how keenly he appreciated the termination of the sedentary life he had been leading these last days. He looked good for about another fifty miles at the same pace, but the sight of us gave him pause. He stopped, looked and listened. Then, as our familiar odour reached his nostrils, he threw his whole soul into a cry of ecstasy. He bounded at Jeeves as if contemplating licking his face, but was checked by the latter's quiet dignity. Jeeves views the animal kingdom with a benevolent eye and is the first to pat its head and offer it a slice of whatever is going, but he does not permit it to lick his face.

So pervasive is this level of camping in Wodehouse that the aunts who tyrannize Bertie Wooster and other Wodehouse heroes are widely assumed to spring from life. Because his father served all his working life in Hong Kong, Wodehouse spent much of his youth passed from aunt to aunt while he acquired a British education. The biographer David Jasen argues that Bertie's Aunt Dahlia is a portrait of Wodehouse's Aunt Louisa and that Aunt Agatha is a portrait of his Aunt Mary,[20] and in a letter to Richard Usborne, Wodehouse once agreed that Aunt Mary was the model for Aunt

Agatha.[21] A. P. Ryan has further argued that all figures of authority in Wodehouse are aunts or "aunts disguised" inasmuch as the essence of Wodehouse's books is the successful rebellion of the young against their elders.[22] It is not actually clear that aunts played any traumatic role in the Wodehouse psyche, but the obsession that Wodehouse *seems* to have with their aggressions is an effective barometer of how thoroughly author and narrator coalesce.[23] The fearsomeness of aunts is actually most amusing, most camp, if it is understood as an auctorial whimsy. Is Bertie to be taken at face value when he alleges a weakness in the knees upon hearing that Esmond Haddock has *five* aunts? Or when he reminds himself portentously that it is not aunts that matter in life but the courage one brings to them? Courage nearly fails him (or so he leads the reader to believe) when he encounters Dame Daphne spraying insecticide in the rose garden of Deverill Hall. "It was plain that for some reason I had fallen in her estimation to approximately the level of a green-fly," he observes. She toys ominously the meanwhile with the trigger of her syringe.

The coalescence of Wodehouse and Bertie on this level of camp humor raises important questions for the entire series of novels. Is Bertie really the "mentally negligible" person that Jeeves once pronounces him or is he a poseur, a Wodehousian alter ego? Does he, in fact, possess a covert appreciation of exactly the kind of foolishness that readers esteem in the novels? Is he an emotionally quiescent man, like Wodehouse, because he will allow neither cynicism nor satiety to compromise his pose of elaborately inflected innocence? In short, is Bertie himself a camp? Surely he manifests a camp's sense of anticlimax when he systematizes the six varieties of hangover as the Broken Compass, the Sewing Machine, the Comet, the Atomic, the Cement Mixer, and the Gremlin Boogie. And surely he manifests a camp's appreciation of situational absurdity when he avers that the Woosters resemble "those Red Indians who, while getting cooked to a crisp at the stake, never failed to be the life and soul of the party." The possibility that his witlessness is a sham opens intriguing vistas. He may seem a Philistine when he remarks that Shakespeare would have admired Emmeline Deverill for her soliloquies at table, but he may also be playing at Philistinism in order to mock Emmeline. The lunatic digression that seems the measure of his mind is often understandable as a ploy. When Corky complains bitterly that the aunts think her a scarlet woman, he remarks blithely, "I've often wondered about that scarlet woman. Was she scarlet all over, or was it just that her face was red?" Corky is effectively kept at a distance. His elaborate ignorance seems oftentimes a defense against emotional involvement. On one occasion he alludes to himself as "a sensitive plant" and Madeline Bassett is dangerously moved. "You know your Shelley, Bertie," she murmurs. "Oh, am I?" he responds.[24]

More than anything else, Bertie's use of the familiar quotation suggests that he is a camp. Such quotations are Jeeves's stock-in-trade, of course, and in the ongoing contest between master and valet Bertie scores off Jeeves repeatedly by his failure to treat literary tags reverentially. Such one-upmanship is funny if he doesn't know what he is doing, but funnier if he does; it is gamesome and blithe if Jeeves is his audience, but an intriguing *self*-entertainment when he is not. The reader is a privileged auditor and Jeeves an implied auditor when Bertie greets a fine morning with the thought that "if God wasn't in His heaven and all right with the world, these conditions prevailed as near as made no matter." Surely he is guying Jeeves when he ostensibly confuses "an eye like Mars" with "an eye like Ma's" and inquires, "What's that thing of Shakespeare's about someone having an eye like Mother?" Many occasions on which he does not *apparently* realize that Jeeves is quoting or on which he is *apparently* unable to recognize a quotation can be understood as similar attempts to flap his unflappable manservant. At a particularly bad moment for Bertie, Jeeves quotes Marcus Aurelius to the effect that all private misfortune has its place in the destiny of the universe. Bertie is able on a later occasion to quote the relevant passage in its entirety, but he affects at the moment a contentious naiveté:

> I breathed a bit stentorously.
> "He said that, did he?"
> "Yes, sir."
> "Well, you can tell him from me he's an ass."

It is not necessary to read *The Mating Season* or any other novel in the series as camp in order to enjoy the Bertie Wooster burble, but the comedy is more insouciant for the additional level of auctorial play that such a reading discerns. In an illustrative passage, Corky sees Bertie battle-scarred from a misadventure with Madeline and is moved to exclaim, "Bertie! My lamb! What have you been doing to yourself? You look like—" "Something the cat brought in?" Bertie suggests helpfully, ever ready with a cliché. "I was going to say something excavated from Tutunkhamen's tomb," she counters innocently. So much is assuredly comedy. But the exchange of imbecilic clichés is elevated to the level of camp improvisation when Jeeves takes exception in his turn to Bertie's appearance. Bertie challenges him, "Say it. I look like something the cat found in Tutunkhamen's tomb, do I not?" Immediately, Wodehouse is off via Bertie into further improvisation:

> "I would not go so far as that, sir, but I have unquestionably seen you more *soigné.*"
>
> It crossed my mind for an instant that with a little thought one might throw together something rather clever about "way down upon the *soigné* river," but I was too listless to follow it up.

Wodehouse's own career as a librettist and his considerable fondness for American songs are inextricably a part of the flourish, and the infectious delight of both author and narrator in Bertie's poor wordplay is a fine, paradoxical counterpoint to Bertie's supposed lassitude.

Bertie Wooster Sees It Through (1954)

Bertie Wooster Sees It Through (better titled in England *Jeeves and the Feudal Spirit*) finds Bertie the proud possessor of a mustache. Jeeves and Aunt Dahlia agree that the growth is frightful, but not so Florence Craye, and when she asks Stilton Cheesewright to grow a similar adornment, Stilton suspects that Bertie once again has designs upon Florence. Indeed, he threatens to break Bertie's spine in precisely three places should an occasion warrant. His suspicions deepen when Florence inveigles Bertie to take her to a disreputable nightclub, for the club is raided that evening, Bertie brought before Stilton's uncle for arraignment, and his assignation with Florence made public knowledge. Stilton makes clear that he would break Bertie's spine in *four* places except that Bertie denies the allegation categorically and insists the magistrate has confused him with someone else. Prudence dictates a withdrawal from the lists, but Bertie is ordered by Aunt Dahlia to Brinkley Court, where Florence and Stilton are houseguests.

At Brinkley Court Bertie finds Aunt Dahlia entertaining the publisher L. C. Trotter and his wife in hopes that he will buy her financially strapped magazine, *Milady's Boudoir.* So desperate is Aunt Dahlia for funds that as part of the bargain she is ready to let Mrs. Trotter have Anatole, her prized French chef. She has already pawned her valuable pearl necklace, and to conceal that indiscretion from her husband she insists that Bertie stage the burglary of a fake set of pearls before the substitution can be discovered. The result is classically farcical: Bertie mistakes the proper window, climbs a ladder into Florence's bedroom rather than into Aunt Dahlia's, and is discovered hiding in a wardrobe by the indignant Stilton, who swears with a fine sense of mathematical progression to break Bertie's spine in *five* places. Shortly afterward, Bertie manages to steal the pearls he thinks are Aunt Dahlia's only to steal instead the fake pearls of Mrs. Trotter, who is guilty like Aunt Dahlia of having pawned the family jewels without her spouse's consent. As an expert in jewels, Jeeves is able to blackmail Mrs. Trotter into allowing her husband to buy *Milady's Boudoir* without Anatole as part of the bargain. Greatly relieved that Brinkley Court will not suffer the loss of its greatest asset and in ostensible gratitude to Jeeves for his intervention, Bertie shaves off his mustache. His real motive is fear that the mustache will attract more women like Florence Craye.

Although thirty-nine years intervened between the writing of "Extricating Young Gussie," the first Bertie Wooster story, and the publication of *Bertie Wooster Sees It Through,* the latter is as fresh in spirit as the former. Wodehouse perfected the Wooster burble so early in his career and established so definitively that Bertie and his cohorts would be forever young that the lack of real development in the series became an important aspect of its charm. Bertie sheds some of his 1920s slang in later decades, to be sure, but he is forever fixed in his own late twenties, and his talent for blundering remains pristine. In deference to history, two world wars are allowed to transpire in the background of the series, but young men continue to linger over port in the 1950s and to patronize the London clubs widely supposed to have attracted them no longer. In short, the series is formulaic and its world is resolutely Edwardian, as George Orwell noted long ago.[25] What brings life to *Bertie Wooster Sees It Through* and other late entries in the series is the perennially fresh language of mixed metaphors, overripe clichés, and fractured quotations that Wodehouse was expert in putting to the service of mad logic and madder dialogue. Indeed, Wodehouse's incomparable ear for such language was the foundation of his camp art.

In an essay entitled "Wodehouse All the Way," Claud Cockburn suggests that Wodehouse's years of writing in America for mass-circulation periodicals like the *Saturday Evening Post* lent him an outsider's sensitivity to the distinctive words, syntax, and cadences of British English. Wodehouse, he suggests, was "jolted, or boosted, into an awareness of the English language which a man who had never experienced the creative schizophrenia of the partially expatriated might never acquire."[26] There is no way of establishing the validity of Cockburn's theory, but it is important for drawing attention to that combination of an insider's affection and an outsider's perspective that is the key to Wodehouse's camping in novels like *Bertie Wooster Sees It Through*. As I have argued previously, it is in the nature of camp fondly to exaggerate a style to the point of making it seem preposterous; both the indulgent affection and the critical perspective are crucial to its success. Just so, Wodehousian English is a pastiche of dead idioms, uncertain allusions, and inapposite similes and metaphors, the pastiche invigorated by unexpected turns of phrase whose originality functions as a counterweight to the verbal maundering.

Anticipating Jeeves's distaste for his mustache, Bertie allows himself a classic disquisition in this insider/outsider mode:

> You know how it is when two strong men live in close juxtaposition, if juxtaposition is the word I want. Differences arise. Wills clash. Bones of contention pop up and start turning handsprings. No one was more keenly alive than I to the fact that one such bone was scheduled to make its debut the instant I swam into his ken, and mere martinis, I felt, despite their numerous merits, would not be enough to see me through the ordeal that confronted me.

The insiderly note is struck immediately with "You know how it is," and Bertie sustains that note in observing, "No one was more keenly alive than I to the fact," as he invites the reader to identify with him in the world of clear-eyed men and women. In the same way, the starkly dramatic syntax of "Differences arise" and "Wills clash" invites the reader to admire and identify with Bertie's stoical acceptance of the way things are. Or so it may seem. That such heroics are applied to the subject of Bertie's mustache invites the reader to a larger view of the enterprise as intrinsically silly. And it is important to the insider/outsider effect of the passage that Bertie is an active agent of that collapse into silliness. He permits the dramatic phrases "Differences arise" and "Wills clash" to culminate in the statement that "Bones of contention *pop up*" [emphasis mine] as if he were abruptly weary of the heroic manner. When he describes those bones of contention as "turning handsprings," the dead metaphor of a bone disputed by two dogs transforms into a lively skeleton dancing on the grave of Bertie's relationship with Jeeves. "Mere martinis" are marshaled against his "ordeal" in a final stand of the heroic manner, and a lively bone of contention is "scheduled to make its *debut*" [emphasis mine] in the context of a badly fractured allusion to Keats's first poem. In short, Bertie both indulges and critiques his appetite for the cliché, the fractured metaphor, and the other devices that anarchically interact in his sentences.

In describing Florence's first response to his mustache, Bertie again makes available to the reader an objective, outsiderly understanding that transcends the insiderly note he establishes as by ritual:

> "Bertie!" she yipped, shaking from stem to stern. "The moustache! It's *lovely!* Why have you kept this from us all these years? It's wonderful. It gives you such a dashing look. It alters your whole appearance."
>
> Well, after the bad press the old fungus had been getting of late, you might have thought that a rave notice like this would have been right up my street. I mean, while one lives for one's Art, so to speak, and cares little for the public's praise or blame and all that sort of thing, one can always do with something to paste into one's scrapbook, can one not? But it left me cold, particularly in the vicinity of the feet. I found my eye swiveling round to Stilton, to see how he was taking it, and was concerned to note that he was taking it extremely big.
>
> Pique. That's the word I was trying to think of.

It is assuredly possible and even conventional to understand this sort of burble as evidence that Bertie is a simpleton. That Florence "yips" while shaking herself "from stem to stern" like a ship-turned-puppy caught in the rain is a giddy mix of implied metaphors, and it is at the same time devastating evidence of the misogynistic strain that cuts through Bertie's appreciation of women. It is no less devastating evidence of Bertie's indolent life that he thinks of growing a mustache as living for his art. The retard on the word *pique* and Bertie's willingness to let "extremely big" stand together with *pique* testifies, it would seem, to the unregenerate amateurism of his memoirs. But it is equally possible and considerably more fun to understand such apparent naiveté as another instance of Bertie indulging an appetite for ungainly prose with full awareness of his lowbrow taste. The implication in Florence's rhapsodic appreciation that Bertie was unprepossessing until his appearance was wholly altered registers with Bertie *apparently* not at all; yet his subsequent gratitude for her appreciation lacks salt unless it is mock gratitude. The cavalier "old fungus" to describe the hirsute growth, the *one*'s that pretend to objectivity, and the scrapbook for verbal compliments are best understood as tongue-in-cheek references. Anyone who can say, "It left me cold, particularly in the vicinity of the feet" understands the interplay of buried metaphors too well to mix puppies and sailboats inadvertently, and anyone who can describe the awesomely outsize Stilton as "taking it extremely big" while pretending to a momentary lapse in vocabulary must understand full well that he leaves himself open to charges of both misogyny and indolence. And he apparently cares not a whit.

A popular misunderstanding of the Bertie Wooster series sees Jeeves as its central and most comic character, but that role belongs indisputably to Bertie. Nor are Bertie and Jeeves properly understood in the symbiotic roles of naif and straight man, for the insider/outsider doubleness of his point of view establishes Bertie as his own straight man. Jeeves is even absent from the scene for long stretches of *Bertie Wooster Sees It Through* and other narratives with no loss of comic vitality in the texts. The very best Wooster burble is self-contained, a game of writerly ineptitude that Bertie seems to play for his own amusement:

> It is pretty generally recognized in the circles in which he moves that Bertram Wooster is not a man who lightly throws in the towel and admits defeat. Beneath the thingummies of what-d'you-call-it his head, wind and weather permitting, is as a rule bloody but unbowed, and if the slings and arrows of outrageous fortune want to crush his proud spirit, they have to pull their socks up and make a special effort.

Even in reported dialogues with another person, Bertie seems the best, most appreciative audience of his own ineptitude. Often he is covertly mocking the presumption of others in reporting their bad judgment of him. When he objects to exiting a bedroom window without a ladder and to ending his days as a smudge on the lawn, he is in a position to appreciate Florence's appalling indifference. "Well," she says, "you can't make an omelette without breaking eggs." Surely it is for his own amusement that he protests weakly, "It seemed to me the silliest thing I had ever heard a girl say, and I have heard girls say some pretty silly things in my time." Indeed, he affects to have no riposte at hand but a sophomoric "You and your bally omelettes," and his apparently insufficient arsenal of retorts makes Florence's indifference seem the ruder. On an earlier occasion, Florence attempts to compliment him: "Everybody says that though you have a brain like a peahen, you're the soul of kindness and generosity." The indirection and exquisite pacing of his response—of the response, at least, that he alleges—is the purest camp:

> Well, I was handicapped here by the fact that, never having met a peahen, I was unable to estimate the quality of these fowls' intelligence, but she had spoken as if they were a bit short of the gray matter, and I was about to ask her who the hell she meant by "everybody," when she resumed.

Bertie is equally capable of affecting obtuseness to mock the cruelty of one character to another. Sarcastically Florence asks him, "What girl would not be delighted who finds herself unexpectedly free from a man [Stilton] with a pink face and a head that looks as if it had been blown up with a bicycle pump?" The mock solicitude of Bertie's response emphasizes her cruelty by making no obvious attempt to rival its wit—which is, of course, the greater wit:

> I clutched the brow. I am a pretty astute chap, and I could see that this was not the language of love. I mean, if you had heard Juliet saying a thing like that about Romeo, you would have raised the eyebrows in quick concern, wondering if all was well with the young couple.

Behind this Bertie who stands behind the burbling Bertie stands Wodehouse, and on a significant number of occasions Wodehouse intrudes upon Bertie's double role to complicate further the point of view:

> It's an odd thing. I know one or two song writers and have found them among the most cheery of my acquaintances, ready of smile and full of merry quips and so forth. But directly they put pen to paper they never fail to take the dark view. All that We're-drifting-apart-you're-breaking-my-heart stuff, I mean to say. The thing this bird was putting across per megaphone at the moment was about a chap crying into his pillow because the girl he loved was getting married next day, but—and

this was the point or nub—not to him. He didn't like it. He viewed the situation with concern. And the megaphonist was extracting every ounce of juice from the setup.

Some fellows, no doubt, would have taken advantage of this outstanding goo to plunge without delay into what Jeeves calls *medias res,* but I, being shrewd, knew that you have to give these things time to work. So, having ordered kippers and a bottle of what would probably turn out to be rat poison, I opened the conversation on a more restrained note, asking her how the new novel was coming along. Authors, especially when female, like to keep you posted about this.

The claim to know "one or two song writers" and the remark that authors like to keep readers posted about their new novels are effective reminders that Wodehouse is an author of the passage, but the burbling Bertie is an author too, his manner unmistakable in the impossibly awkward hyphenation of "We're-drifting-apart-you're-breaking-my-heart" and the allusion to "what Jeeves calls *medias res.*" The more effaced Bertie Wooster can also be distinguished, especially in the line "he viewed the situation with concern," which echoes George and Ira Gershwin's classic song "A Foggy Day" (in the wake of a reference to the scent of kippered herring hanging over the establishment "like a fog") without appeal to Jeeves for verification or correction. Such individual strands of authorship cannot always be untangled in this manner, however. The authorship of either one of the two Berties *or* of Wodehouse is implied by the voguish slang, used with just sufficient ineptitude and aggression to suggest mental vacuity *or* mockery. The deprecatory *stuff* and the gender-awkward *bird* are especially fine.

This entanglement of three narrational personae in *Bertie Wooster Sees It Through* suggests that it and similar novels in the series owe a debt to the interactive levels of wit in the comedy of manners as well as to the revolving-door bedrooms and inconsequential amorality of French farce. The rich play of country against London manners, of servants' against masters' mores, and of female against male sensitivities leads by a kind of osmosis to the metaphysically richer play of the Wodehouse persona upon the Bertie Wooster persona who is his effaced narrator, and to their combined play upon the Bertie Wooster who burbles unself-consciously. If the novels sacrifice little of their innocence to such sophisticated play, it is because their innocence is never anything more than a camp joke. Unlike the novels of E. F. Benson, in which innocence is occasionally real, and unlike the novels of Ivy Compton-Burnett, in which a marginal innocence is threatened by all manner of more-than-camp darkness, it is the distinctive camping of Wodehouse's novels that their burble of innocence is celebrated with sweet unreason in the sunlight of an eternal spring.

7

The Palette Darkened: Ivy Compton-Burnett

The novels of Ivy Compton-Burnett have possibly inspired a greater range of literary comparison than those of any other writer. It is most commonly said of them that her characters inhabit the country of Jane Austen—that they are as socially restricted as the inhabitants of Mansfield Park or Highbury, that they live the same lives *en famille* that Austen's characters live, and that their disposition to speak plainly, affectedly, or in sophisticated understatement categorizes them intellectually as much as such habits of speech categorize General Tilney and Elizabeth Bennet.[1] Somewhat confusingly, Compton-Burnett's characters are said almost as often to inhabit the world of Greek tragedy and to suffer its distinctive cruelties and ironies.[2] The author's apparent stoicism and the terrible acts of passion that occur between chapters of her novels are thought to link her in a special way to Euripides.[3]

Compton-Burnett's novels are also thought a fusion of late-Victorian and Edwardian sensibilities, inasmuch as all except one of them are set between 1888 and 1902, the year 1901 and the accession of Edward VII to the British throne serving as their gravitational center. "I do not feel that I have any real or organic knowledge of life later than about 1910," she told her companion Margaret Jourdain in 1945.[4] Yet for many readers, Compton-Burnett's novels evoke the modern world. Elizabeth Bowen professed in 1941 that "to read in these days a page of Compton-Burnett dialogue is to think of the sound of glass being swept up, one of these London mornings after a blitz."[5] Raymond Mortimer has linked her writings to the postimpressionism of Cézanne;[6] Edward Sackville-West, to the cubism of the early Picasso.[7] Charles Burkhart emphasizes her interest in the existential gap between men and material reality in order to suggest her affinity with Samuel Beckett,[8] and the novelist Anthony Powell emphasizes her view of ironic despair against a background of humdrum circumstances in order to link her to Harold Pinter.[9] Nathalie Sarraute views her as a forerunner of the *nouvelle roman* in France.[10]

In the face of such varied understandings of the novels, can it be possible that Compton-Burnett is also a camp humorist? Certainly her novels are less intentionally camp than those of any other writer treated in these pages. One suspects, indeed, that Compton-Burnett would not have been pleased to find herself in sequence with E. F. Benson and P. G. Wodehouse, for she was obviously a serious woman who wrote novels that she thought realistic about the tyrannies of family and quasi-familial life. "My writing does not seem to me as 'stylised' as it apparently is," she once complained.[11] Neither did she like to think of herself as the camp icon she became in Cecil Beaton's 1947 photograph, in which she is framed by shieldlike firescreens while gazing directly at the camera in a composition severe, hieratic, and sinister.[12]

But what do her reservations matter? Like any species of humor, the instinct for camp can be unconscious—even a finer thing than it might otherwise be for having escaped auctorial intention. Indeed, humor can exist only in an audience's understanding of something intended quite seriously. It seems beyond question today that Beaton's portrait captures something fundamental about Compton-Burnett that is equally fundamental to some of her novels: a grotesque stiltedness; a *camp* stiltedness, ultimately, that both accommodates and disaccommodates melodrama. Although in some ways they resist assimilation into the genre, novels like *More Women Than Men, Daughters and Sons,* and *A Family and a Fortune* hold an important place in the tradition of the camp narrative.

More Women Than Men (1933)

More Women Than Men is the first of Compton-Burnett's major novels, a wonderfully sordid tale of jealousy, sexual intrigue, and murder in a girls' school. The institution is dominated by its owner and headmistress, Josephine Napier. Her husband Simon assists in her work, and her adopted son Gabriel lives with them, although he is increasingly eager to live an independent life. Gabriel's acknowledged father is Josephine's brother, Jonathan Swift, who gave up his infant son for adoption after his wife died in young motherhood. Or so Jonathan alleges. He lives now in genteel poverty with a young man named Felix Bacon. Badgered by his father to act like a responsible adult, Felix accepts a position as a drawing master on Josephine's faculty, but not to his father's satisfaction. Lord Bacon considers the position womanish, like his son.

When a destitute woman named Elizabeth Giffard and her daughter Ruth arrive at the school looking for employment, Josephine hires Elizabeth as her housekeeper and creates a position for Ruth as a teacher. Ostentatiously kind, she protests that she welcomes them as old friends, not employees, even though she is aware that Elizabeth and Simon were once lovers and even though she concealed the news of Elizabeth's widowhood from Simon until she was safely married to him herself. Tragedy waits upon the rashly conceived ménage. Entering the library one day as Elizabeth is steadying a ladder for Simon, Josephine startles the pair, Elizabeth involuntarily jerks the ladder, and Simon falls to his death. Some months later, Gabriel announces that he wants to marry Elizabeth's daughter despite Josephine's objections. "You will take my daughter's lover, as you took mine?" asks Elizabeth, melodramatically.

Josephine takes more than Ruth's lover when she deliberately exposes the young bride to a draft while pretending to nurse her through pneumonia. Miss Rosetti, a senior mistress, witnesses the murderous deed and in exchange for her silence is offered the chance to buy a partnership in the school. Miss Rosetti has her own secrets: she is Gabriel's real mother, not dead at all, and she is the anonymous donor of a benefaction that enabled Gabriel to marry Ruth. In the increasing confusion, Josephine finds her maternal affection for Gabriel evolving into an affection for Felix that is both maternal and erotic. To be rid of her son, she blithely encourages Gabriel to marry Helen Keats, a young woman on her staff, only to be foiled when Felix marries Helen in an inexplicable submission to a deathbed wish of his father that he should embrace a conventional mode of life. A letter accidentally discovered reveals to Josephine that Miss Rosetti is the mother of her adopted son and the anonymous donor of his benefaction; Gabriel also discovers the facts. How can he live under one roof with his biological mother, his adoptive mother, and his mother-in-law? He goes to live with Jonathan instead, taking Felix's place in the all-male household. Concomitantly, Josephine and Miss Rosetti settle down rather too cozily to the running of their school in a legal and apparently loving partnership.

As the foregoing summary suggests, the plot of *More Women*

Than Men is built of overripe Victoriana. The reader is treated to an impoverished woman arriving out of the night with portentous secrets; to an illegitimate son discovering that his allegedly deceased mother has watched another woman raise him for twenty years; and to a woman of daunting self-control giving way to her feelings in one, murderous instant. What could be more of a Victorian cliché than Felix's submission to his father's deathbed entreaty or the accidentally discovered letter that reveals a terrible family secret? So palpable is the Victorian ambience of the novel that Miss Rosetti emblemizes danger for no other reason than that she was born of Italian parents and brought up—*quelle horreur!*—in France. Like good Victorian children, the students in the school contrive rarely to be seen and never to be heard. Josephine's administration of the school evokes in a special way the claustrophobic coziness of a Victorian parlor, as when she rebukes Mrs. Chattaway, one of her teachers, for betraying a small unhappiness in her profession:

> "A feeling of that kind, even if not fostered, does unfit you for your work," said Josephine in a serious tone. "But may I pay you a compliment, and say that I do not think you can have it? I have watched you—No, no! No more and no less than it has been my duty to watch you—and I think that the feeling was a part of the disturbance of your life, when you first joined us—Believe me, I saw it with great sympathy—and that it has since vanished. Am I not right?"

The deaths of Simon and Ruth and the flight of Gabriel from the maternal nest suggest that Josephine's concern for the well-being of those around her is the suffocating solicitude of a Victorian parent. The teachers' common room is theoretically their own preserve, but Josephine visits the room many times in the role of materfamilias, each time effusively apologetic for the intrusion. The teachers attempt irony with her ("You should hesitate to enter a room in your own house"), analogy ("I have only just brought myself to do it," proclaims Felix), and finally embarrassed silence, but nothing deflects Josephine from assuring herself volubly of her welcome and of the teachers' recognition of her great solicitude for them. Such pro forma gushes of feeling are Josephine's most irritating, most suffocating habit. One of the teachers misses a train back to the school after her holiday and is treated to quaint reassurance: "It is not at all the duty of trains to us, to go on while we are waiting. We cannot be expected to do more than arrive and wait." When Elizabeth apologizes for bitter words that she has said in the past, Josephine says patronizingly, "Well, be thankful you said them to someone who knew you could not mean them."

Against such Victorian clichés of plotting and speech making, the author sets modern inconsequentialness. In the light of day, Elizabeth's dark secrets are only about shabby human failures; the mother who has stood apart while her son was raised by another woman confesses that she has never regretted standing apart; and an undetected murderess is allowed to play at a widow's grief until she wearies of the role. In contradistinction to attitudes that had surfaced in the prosecution of Radclyffe Hall five years before the novel's publication, the author treats homosexuality as especially inconsequential. Lesbian sexuality is a discreet aura in the teachers' common room and spills into the headmistress's office without constituting in any way a danger to the school. Felix and Jonathan have been lovers for some twenty years without endangering either their own or the public weal and without incapacitating Felix for heterosexual marriage. Felix's ingenuousness seems in many ways the pattern of Compton-Burnett's own attitude toward homosexuality. "I cannot imagine any useful and self-respecting person of either sex wishing to belong to the other," says Josephine, with Victorian prudery in her voice. "Neither can I, a person of that kind," Felix counters mildly. When Jonathan sets up house with Gabriel he is delighted to have found a replacement for Felix, and of the potentially incestuous cohabitation he says, "Ah, that is the natural tie." "Of course it is," responds Felix. "But you wanted an unnatural one."[13]

As Felix's remarks serve to illustrate, Compton-Burnett's most shocking deployment of the inconsequential is in her dialogue. In counterpoint to Josephine's fulsome mode of expressing herself, she proffers a mode of speech in which other characters speak without fear of consequence the sort of thing that is generally thought unsayable—the sort of thing that belongs to unconscious awareness inasmuch as it seems anterior to the censoring function of the superego. Helen asks Felix if Jonathan was crushed by the news of his engagement to Mary, and Felix answers, "Yes; I almost thought it would kill him. I suppose I was just going to let it. Engaged people are supposed to be selfish, and I think this shows that they are." Understood according to the traditions of Victorian propriety and novelistic realism, the speech is shockingly cold-blooded, but understood in a Freudian paradigm it is intelligent, honest, and dispassionately insightful. Nathalie Sarraute suggests that such remarks exist "on the fluctuating frontier that separates conversation from sub-conversation."[14] The point is important, for it was Compton-Burnett's genius to subvert the high-flown rhetoric of Victorian unctuousness with the subconversation of modern psychological awareness. Conventional passages of description, auctorial commentary, and the tedious business of dialogue tags she greatly reduces from the norm in order to allow the counterpoint of conversation and subconversation a starkly dramatic play.

The starkness of that conversational counterpoint imparts a fine edge to moments of honesty not otherwise impressive. Interviewing her teachers one by one as they return from their holidays, Josephine embarks on treacherous waters with Miss Rosetti, just after dealing with Miss Luke:

> "I hope you have escaped [the] experience of a crowded carriage?"
>
> "No, I have not escaped it. I have been sitting upright in the middle of one row of people, and opposite another," said the newcomer, in a deep, dragging voice, a movement of her shoulders implying that the posture she mentioned was unnatural.
>
> "Well, I suppose we have no reason for objecting to the presence of our fellow creatures," said Josephine, continuing in Miss Luke's line.
>
> "I had reasons for objecting to the presence of these creatures. And I don't know why they were my fellows: I saw no basis of fellowship."

On the one hand, Josephine's upholding an ideal of democratic fellowship is creditable; she even implements the ideal by talking in a friendly way with a subordinate. On the other hand, Miss Rosetti's disdain for the ideal lacks subtlety and wit; only her honesty commends it. But the force of the contrast between Josephine's conventional geniality and Miss Rosetti's honest petulance imparts a considerable distinction to the latter. Indeed, the reader tends to doubt that Miss Rosetti's words are actually vocalized. They are too bravely uncompliant in a woman for whom compliance makes possible her livelihood. They seem the subtext of unheard, more innocuous remarks in a conversation that has been edited beyond conventional language to a truer communication. In such an exchange of remarks—by no means always the norm—Miss Rosetti seems one of those Compton-Burnett characters described by V. S. Pritchett as speaking "like brilliant skeletons come out of their closets."[15]

In the course of the narrative, a number of such subtexts seem to displace surface texts that are effectively lost to the reader, just as the author's use of famous names—Keats, Ros(s)etti, Bacon, Jonathan Swift—seems to hint at a lost level of literary analogy. Presented with a wedding gift by his students, Felix announces that their gift is more meaningful to him than their good wishes because without the gift the wishes are facile. Or so he is *said* to announce. When Josephine thereafter congratulates him on a charming speech, readers may suspect that they have read what Felix would have liked to say rather than the words actually uttered on that ceremonious occasion. "Opinions differ so much more on speeches [than on marriages]," Felix responds to Josephine; "I am sorry for the hint of effort about mine; I had no time to make it spontaneous." Does he actually say such words to his employer, a woman whose "spontaneous" speeches are famous for their elaborate preparation? Perhaps, but Josephine does not seem to have heard the words recorded on the page, rather some other words, when she answers, "Do you know, I find it odd to think of you as a family man?" Again, does Felix actually greet parents of incoming students whose work he has never seen with assurances that their daughters have artistic talent beyond the ordinary? Since the headmistress is standing beside him at the moment it seems likely that the recorded words are a parodic subtext of more conventional greetings. Emblematic of this tendency for subtexts to displace surface texts is a scene in which Josephine replies from outside a door to criticisms that Ruth avers she was not meant to hear. "I hardly understand this talking according to whether or no the talk is heard," Josephine complains. Gabriel agrees: "We hardly understand this talking to someone neither here nor elsewhere. It is an unbearable method of communication."

Among themselves, the teachers may often seem to converse with the headmistress's own decorum, even to slip into inanities, but a subtextual reading of their conversation suggests barbed irony and bitterness as the truer locution. Fresh from her "welcome-back" interview with Josephine, Mrs. Chattaway says with apparent vacuity, "I hardly liked to appear before Mrs. Napier, kind though she is. I think she was especially kind today." The careful reader will note that *kind* may carry invisible quotation marks and constitute an allusion to the manneredness of Josephine's kindness—that it may even be quietly sarcastic. In light of Josephine's high-handed show of virtue, the sarcasm would certainly be appreciable. "I noticed that her standard was high," observes Helen Keats in a—catty?—reference to Josephine's continual flying of her standard. "It is wonderful how she enters into the lives of all the people about her," remarks Miss Chattaway in turn; "If I had known it when I first came, I should have had a happier beginning." Does her *wonderful* mean *astonishing?* Her *happier, more successful?* "I suppose she forgot to tell you," says Helen insouciantly, and at that point Miss Rosetti laughs boldly; Miss Luke, a little nervously—their laughter making clear the disingenuousness of the whole exchange. Women so practiced in concealing their meaning underneath surface decorum might be thought inevitably to step over "the fluctuating frontier that separates conversation from sub-conversation."

At her best, Compton-Burnett shapes her characters' ironies and subtextual honesties into configurations that evoke the brilliance of Oscar Wilde in his stage comedies. "My father should have had a daughter," observes Felix at the start of a typically Wildean passage. "Does he wish he had had a daughter?" asks Jonathan.

> "Yes. He says he would have found one a consolation. He says too, that I might be a woman, for all the differences he can see. That seems to show that I have tried to be a comfort to him."

The subject of working for one's living inspires Felix to wonderfully Wildean nonsense:

> "I never think about people's work. Work is a thing I do not like to think about. It is odd that my father always connects me with it. He can hardly separate the two ideas."
>
> "Does he suggest anything definite?"
>
> "That I should save him the expense of an agent, and the discredit of having a son who will not live in his house. I don't mean that he actually suggests the whole of that."
>
> "He does not sound addicted to work himself."
>
> "Of course he is not addicted to work. Please do not speak unsuitably about my father."

Like Algernon Moncrieff or Cecily Cardew, Felix is not self-consciously clever when he says such things. His wit is simply an honesty uncorrupted by the censoring superego and by Victorian habits of linguistic subterfuge. Indeed, the passage suggests Wildean nonsense only for readers who live less completely than Felix in the sphere of moral inconsequence and therefore find mildly shocking such freedom from cant. Wilde *knew* he was being shocking, of course, but Compton-Burnett was more genuinely a believer in moral inconsequence than both Wilde and the majority of her readers, and she may have intended to depict nothing more than candor.

Indeed, it would not be accurate to suggest that Compton-Burnett posits the same world of moral inconsequence that Oscar Wilde posits. *The Importance of Being Earnest* is a work of relatively pure camp inasmuch as it takes a holiday from the real world and quashes all its possible undercurrents of social, psychological, and moral seriousness. But Compton-Burnett's refusal in *More Women Than Men* to treat homosexuality in any censorious way has rhetorical relevance in the real world. So, too, have her recognition that working women are tyrannized in one of the few professions open to them, and her openness to Freudian understandings. The murder of Ruth, the sudden sexual metamorphosis of Felix, and the sight of Josephine and Miss Rosetti locked in their first embrace are shocks "as trim and tidy as a handgrenade," as Pamela Hansford Johnson has said,[16] and they are shocks beyond the ability of Wilde's characters to withstand. The elements of melodrama are permitted to retain much of their original force in Compton-Burnett, in other words. What lends *More Women Than Men* a camp dimension is not any significant leave-taking of the real world but the absurd trimness and tidiness of which Johnson speaks. The economy of presentation implicit in the mesh of text and subtext, in the pointedness of the dialogue, and in the too-easy interchange of erotic roles has the effect of attenuating the luridness of the story—of treating the consequential in an inconsequential way without quite rendering it negligible. Josephine is a camp figure as she egregiously upstages Gabriel in both his happiness and his grief because the reader knows she is an actress so carried away by her role that she can no longer distinguish between emotions real and counterfeit. She is also an authentic Victorian villainess.

Daughters and Sons (1937)

Daughters and Sons is a novel about three generations of an English family that share an ample but understaffed country home and a barely sufficient income for their needs. At the head of the family is eighty-four-year-old Sabine Ponsonby, a woman who gives herself autocratic license to speak evil of everyone and to accept instruction in charity from no one. Her son John is approximately fifty years old, a once-popular novelist no longer able to command a public, and her daughter Hetta is a forty-eight-year-old spinster who has functioned self-importantly as John's secretary and housekeeper since his wife died in childbirth leaving him with three daughters and two sons, all of them living at home. In order of age, the children are Clare, twenty-five years old; Frances, twenty-four; Chilton, eighteen; Victor, seventeen; and Muriel, eleven. The household is completed by a series of governesses for Muriel (in sequence, Miss Bunyan, Miss Hallam, Miss Blake, and then Miss Bunyan again), and a tutor for the boys (Alfred Marcon).

Two generations of sons and daughters are not easy to maintain in the perfect, hierarchical subjection thought suitable in Edwardian households, but Sabine and Hetta manage the trick by continually reminding the youngest generation that it is inexperienced, untrained, and dependent for its minimal comforts upon Sabine's and John's incomes and upon the two women's combined household management. In the face of such tyranny, the young can only cling to the truer and meaner facts of their situation, which they observe continually in sotto voce commentaries, raised to full voice only when their elders demand it. Typically, Sabine pronounces Clare dull-complexioned, dull-mannered, and dull-faced. "I do not know what your father will think of you," she concludes dismissively. "You should know," responds Clare quietly; "You have outlined the impression I produce." "Do not be self-conscious and conceited, girl," returns Sabine. "Self-conscious you may have made me," murmurs her grandchild; "conceited is not so likely."

The plot of the novel revolves upon Frances's winning a literary prize of two thousand pounds for a first novel that she has published under the name of the governess Edith Hallam from fear of her father's professional jealousy. One thousand pounds of the prize she sends anonymously to her father, and when Sabine intercepts a letter from Frances's publisher to the cognominal Edith Hallam, she concludes that the governess is not only the successful novelist and the source of the thousand pounds, but a potential source of more wealth. She quickly persuades John to marry her. Edith has no wish to displace Hetta in her role as majordomo, but Hetta feels her position eroded by the marriage and allows the family to think she has drowned herself in a nearby river—a melodramatic feint whose cruelty the family does not readily forgive. At a subsequent dinner party, designed to show the neighbors a family restored to harmony, Hetta therefore denounces them all: Sabine for opening Edith's mail, John for marrying Edith for her alleged money, Frances and Edith for conspiring to deceive John. Sabine quietly expires during the tirade, giving rise to a new crisis when it is mistakenly rumored that she has left all her money to the boys' tutor, Alfred Marcon. Alfred announces that he intends to accept fully half the legacy, but the novel ends with the reading of a will leaving only a small bequest to Alfred and the bulk to members of the family, whose youngest sons and daughters can look forward to a life somewhat more free than it had been of hierarchical tyranny.

In the way of Compton-Burnett's novels, *Daughters and Sons* reprises several of the ingredients of *More Women Than Men*. Both novels feature parent-child relationships rendered askew by a father who hands over the rearing of his children to a female relation, and both depict terrible abuses of power by those women. In both, claims to self-sacrificing devotion and financial hardship do not justify victimization of the children, although the children are in both cases almost too old to be credible as victims. Compton-Burnett takes a grim view of the exploitation of governesses in *Daughters and Sons* that recalls her view of the exploitation of teachers in *More Women Than Men,* and she permits herself a pseudoallusive, unsystematic use of names like Sabine, Charity, Bunyan, Chaucer, and Jane Seymour that recalls her use in the earlier novel of names like Keats, Ros(s)etti, Bacon, and Jonathan Swift. There is no murder in *Daughters and Sons,* but there is a sham suicide; no blatant homosexuality, but a notable shortage of married couples and a whiff of incest; no actual illegitimacy, but many and varied ruptures of parental bonds. In both, an anonymous benefaction is an important catalyst of the plot.[17]

What is conspicuously absent from *Daughters and Sons* is the stylized graciousness of a Josephine Napier, for the Ponsonbys take their stylistic cues from Sabine, who exempts herself entirely from conventional politeness. "Are they never going?" she is wont to murmur in the hearing of guests. Conspicuously absent, too, is Compton-Burnett's characteristic displacement of surface texts with subtexts. Indeed, characters speak their entire thoughts in *Daughters and Sons* without significant recourse to subterfuge, only to lowered tones of voice. In such respects, the novel represents an advance in the author's art. Effectively, Compton-Burnett trusts to the naked rendering of family conversation in *Daughters and Sons* without the heightening effects of stylistic contrast on the one hand or "brilliant skeletons come out of their closets" on the other.[18] This is not to say that the method of the novel is realism. The characters talk with unnatural lucidity and tireless sensitivity to the shifting moods of family discourse as if they were disengaged observers of the scene, whereas they are in actuality observing themselves and the family to which they belong. The effect is the painterly one of lending a realistic composition unnatural luminosity and suggesting thereby that even its clichés bespeak an implacable truth.

When Sabine, for instance, tells Miss Bunyan that she is not to consider herself part of the family, Victor says, "Grandma, you are ruder than is human. I almost admire it." "I do not," observes Clare immediately. Between them, Victor and Clare vocalize polarized, vaguely schematic attitudes that might be adopted toward Sabine's temerity, and, incredibly, they do so without apparent fear of her ire. Indeed, they manifest a commensurate temerity that undercuts the implied moral bases of their respective judgments when both seem to imply that Sabine should not consider herself part of the *human* family. That something atavistic in human nature tends to admire monsters of egotism who transcend human acculturation is a recognized fact, and Victor speaks for that admiration. That an educated moral sense can both recognize and scorn that admiration is equally the case, and Clare speaks for that point of view. Sabine's ignoring both her grandchildren's remarks implies a third point of view—that their views are negligible in view of her right as an octogenarian and as their grandmother to say exactly what she pleases. But all three points of view are rendered sterile by their conjunction, and their ramifications are mute in view of the common audacity of utterance. The "implacable truth" of the scene is its depiction of three persons unproductively at loggerheads. What they say and even the disengagement with which they say it tend to be nullified in the wonder of their saying it at all.

Such moments are many. One thinks of Frances's unnaturally disengaged wit in asking her siblings the thoroughly practical question, "Shall we be in time for luncheon, or a little late? Which will cause us less humiliation?" Believing Hetta a suicide, Sabine harangues her assembled grandchildren intemperately: "You did not spare my daughter. You did nothing for Hetta; you would not care if she was dead. You only think of the five of yourselves. You think you are the world." Clare responds blandly, "Well, that is not unnatural, Grandma. We have had to be our own world. We have had no other." "Smartness, smartness," grumbles Sabine, but it is not smartness so much as a sense of fact that Clare counterpoises to her grandmother's invective, with the effect of neutralizing the scene's emotional acidity. Again and again, the adult grandchildren express sentiments so unnaturally calm and lucid as to seem archetypal truths. "Things do not stand the test of years," observes Frances, "certainly not homes." Reflecting on Hetta's relationship with John, she says, "The tragedy is giving up your life to someone who will not repay you with his own. Finding that he will not give you any part of his prime, in return for the whole of yours." The grandchildren believe in nothing, apparently, not their family, their futures, least of all in some overarching benevolence. Disbelief is the source of their gift for the dispassionate utterance that keeps counsel with despair. Of Hetta's attendance at church, Frances says, "If she were religious, she would not go. She would have thought about her religion and lost it." "We must cultivate the courage of despair," admonishes Victor.

A series of subplots that resonate with the main plot deepens the reader's sense of being privy to an unnatural illumination of the world's fundamental arrangements—the arrangements of marriage in particular. In a carefully understressed development that might otherwise have been sentimental, the governess Miss Bunyan writes home, hinting coyly that she might marry into the Ponsonby family:

> I am already "my dear" [with Sabine]. Her son, my pupil's father, is returning to-night, John Ponsonby, the novelist. Mrs Ponsonby seems to think that as members of intellectual professions we should be thrown together. I will leave this letter open in case of more to say to-morrow. At the moment my pillow invites.

That the poor woman fantasizes marrying into the family is sad, for it suggests the depth of her need for some human attachment, however uncongenial; that her successor is offered the family position she fails to achieve is pitilessly ironic; and that Sabine should covertly open the letter and promptly exclude Miss Bunyan from the dinner table in the name of family life is wantonly cruel. The narrator quips that feminine endurance is said to be formidable, but Sabine manages nonetheless to drive Miss Bunyan away into the unwelcoming arms of her uncle, the local vicar, himself so eager to marry that he proposes serially to Miss Hallam and Miss Blake and is finally accepted by Hetta after her fall from family grace. In kindred developments, Clare accepts Alfred Marcon as part of the arrangement that he would claim half rather than the whole of Sabine's legacy, and she is subsequently betrothed to a Mr. Rutland, prompting Edith to remark, "It is fortunate that the match is as suitable as it is, considering she always accepts the men."

Edith's remark is telling, for what emerges from all these matrimonial endeavors is a suggestion that marriage is the desperate last remedy for men and women in intolerable family situations of all kinds—for Alfred Marcon, suffering the kindness of his uncle and aunt; for the vicar, suffering the enforced companionship of his niece; for Hetta, suffering pathologically from incestuous desire; for the several governesses, suffering a reluctance of their families to take them in; and for the Ponsonby grandchildren, suffering with desperate fortitude their egregious elders. Indeed, there is no variety of family life or nonlife that seems remotely tolerable in the world of *Daughters and Sons,* and all of them are too sordid for polite exposure. The grandchildren's unnaturally dispassionate observations are their necessary self-assertion in a family structure that denies them a right to assertiveness, certainly; but they are also immemorial stratagems of concealment, serving to hide in plain sight the unspeakable oppressions of family life. "Isn't it wonderful that they *are* hidden?" chirps the kindly Charity Marcon, adding, "We really don't deserve it."

As with *More Women Than Men,* then, it would be a mistake to think of *Daughters and Sons* as taking leave of the real world. Compton-Burnett imposes on a psychopathic dimension of family life the traditions of literary and social reticence, refusing both to sensationalize modes of human behavior that beguile the modern mind and to affect that they do not exist.[19] Must—*can?*—the reader distinguish between the author's reticence as a habit of her Edwardian upbringing and as a habit of understatement that functions in the cause of irony? It sufficed Compton-Burnett that her plainness of idiom preserved human dignity, and it must suffice the contemporary reader that such plainness is no less a tradition of manners than a tradition of wit.

No scene in the novel is more indicative of Compton-Burnett's ability to probe the psychopathic with simultaneous reticence and wit than that in which several members of the family discuss Miss Blake's refusal of Dr. Chaucer:

> "I think a proposal is often an insult," said Hetta in a dreamy tone, her hands again behind her head. "I always wonder women do not see it. But they do not. And I daresay it is a good thing. The world has to go on."
>
> "Miss Blake's perceptions were above the average," said Clare.
>
> "And the world has received a check," said Chilton. "Muriel is again at the beginning."
>
> Muriel burst into laughter at the reminder of her late humour.
>
> "I did not mean that kind of insult," said Hetta, still dreamily.
>
> "It is a good thing she is going," said Sabine in an ordinary tone. "Whatever Dr. Chaucer meant, it was less than she thought, and he is glad of his escape. It means he is in the mood for marriage and does not meet a woman to his mind."
>
> "The proposal was clearly an insult," said Frances.

In the governing context of this passage, what Hetta seems to mean by her criticism of marriage proposals is that they presuppose women wish to surrender their independence to men. But only in her "dreamy," intellectually disengaged state could she fancy such a presumption as insulting, for she longs for a legitimization with anyone of the role she plays in her brother's household. Clare's subsequent observation about Miss Blake's intelligence is open, then, to at least two understandings: first, that Miss Blake saw precisely the insulting situation that Hetta thinks beyond her ken; second, that she saw more facets, both positive and negative, in the proposal than Hetta is capable of seeing, because she is less blinded than Hetta by self-defensive theorizing. In the wake of Clare's artful ambiguity, who knows what Hetta means by her dismissive, markedly delayed, "I did not mean that kind of insult"? Sensitive, perhaps, to the discussion's drift into ambiguity and incoherence, Sabine reestablishes the so-called ordinary tone with a heady dose of relativism. "Whatever Dr. Chaucer meant, it was less than she thought," she pronounces. She goes on to suggest that the flirtatious Dr. Chaucer has not yet met a woman who pleases him.

It is against the background of this gathering incoherence, relativism, and absurdity that Frances closes the discussion by announcing that the proposal is *clearly* an insult. The proposal is clearly an insult only in the immediate light of Sabine's observation that Dr. Chaucer has not yet met a woman to his taste, because that suggests that *Hetta* is not to his taste, which is, of course, the insulting aspect of the vicar's proposal to Miss Blake that *really* offends Hetta, which Frances *knows,* and which knowledge she permits Hetta to *misunderstand* in specious agreement with her original remark. The whole passage is a wonderful tangle of cross-purposed statements that snap elegantly into shape at the end. It suggests, ultimately, a camp rapprochement with reality—with, at least, the multiple realities of sexual frustration, self-delusion, compensatory logic, and familial all-knowingness. The rapprochement is camp because such terrible afflictions of the spirit are not permitted to disturb the poise of its wit, its thematically unsuitable trimness of manner, its tidiness of effect. Like many such passages in *Daughters and Sons,* it permits the reader a momentary belief that disastrously frank badinage might be a viable stay against confusion—a belief fundamental to the camp faith.

A Family and a Fortune (1939)

A Family and a Fortune does not enjoy the critical status of Compton-Burnett's allegedly best novel, *Manservant and Maidservant,*[20] but it is the most highly regarded among those of her novels that are appreciable as camp.[21] It is the story, once again, of an unexpected legacy and a multigenerational family. The legatee is Dudley Gaveston, a bachelor in his early fifties, who inherits two thousand pounds a year upon the death of his godfather. The family is composed of Edgar and Blanche Gaveston and their four children: Justine, who is thirty years old; Mark, twenty-eight; Clement, twenty-six; and Aubrey, fifteen. Dudley Gaveston is Edgar's brother and lives with the family in their large, somewhat moldering house. Impoverished Oliver and Matty Seaton, Blanche's father and sister, are newly resident in a small lodge on the Gaveston property. Matty is attended by a paid companion named Miss Griffin.

The Gavestons are unusually well-behaved for a Compton-Burnett family. Clement is sometimes sullen, Justine is unrelentingly officious, and Edgar is remote from everyone except his brother, but they commit no murders and are not egregiously incestuous. They even abide by the rules of polite behavior. As the younger of the two brothers, Dudley is especially well-behaved, for he has mastered the art of playing second fiddle. His easy intimacy with Edgar is accepted by Blanche without jealousy and is admired extravagantly by Justine, who considers it superior to any other relationship she knows. When Dudley comes unexpectedly into his fortune, the ingrained habit of deference inspires him to distribute the income among the family members, who accept it without awkward demur. They are almost equally graceful when Dudley must retract his largess after he is betrothed to Maria Sloane, a visiting friend of Matty. Occasional misbehavior in the family is on a modest scale. In the most sensational instance, the recently widowed Edgar marries Maria, Dudley's fiancée, but there is no obvious ill will or calculation in his cutting out his brother. That Dudley subsequently leaves the house in a snowstorm and almost dies of pneumonia is an unfortunate consequence of his newly clouded relationship with Edgar, but little more. It does not preclude Edgar's rushing to Dudley's sickbed out of genuine concern for his welfare.

The only evil person in the novel is Matty Seaton, who allows her semi-invalidism to excuse a tyrannical disposition. She exercises especially a tyranny over the long-suffering Miss Griffin, and her cruelty becomes a scandal when she turns Miss Griffin out one snowy evening (the same evening as Dudley's flight into the snow) without benefit of hat or shawl. Because Matty lives in the lodge, her power over the Gavestons is considerably less than her power over Miss Griffin and hardly a threat at all. Indeed, the plot of the novel is largely the story of Matty's laying siege to the main house: her establishing a beachhead there through the introduction of her friend Maria into the family; her insistence on moving into the house after the deaths of Blanche and Oliver; her temporary rule over the household while Maria, Edgar, and Justine hold vigil at Dudley's sickbed; and her presumptive defeat when the three reestablish themselves in the house and ask pointedly about her plans for the future.

A Family and a Fortune is interestingly compared with *More Women Than Men* and *Daughters and Sons* insofar as it reprises their familiar motifs in a less melodramatic story with no Freudian implications. Its family includes still another tyrant, still another emotionally distant father, and still another gaggle of articulate children, but among the many characters only Matty is impelled to the melodramatic gesture. The unnatural candor of conversation within the family illumines once again several tenebrous aspects of late-Victorian and Edwardian morality, but psychological issues have only a referential, not a dramatic presence in the novel. Indeed, there is less of a tendency than in the earlier novels for characters to say the conventionally unsayable—probably because the psychological circumstances with which the characters have to deal are less terrible than before. The art of the earlier novels is the overlaying of a fastidious narrative manner upon a mishmash of skeletons tumbled from a late-Victorian cupboard; the art (and the camp joke) of *A Family and a Fortune* is Compton-Burnett's exercising herself in the same fastidious manner while affecting to know nothing whatsoever of skeletons or cupboards.

Much of the fun of the novel is that trivial developments fatten themselves on complications real and illusory even while they are examined (à la Henry James) for ever-more-precise understandings of motive and impulse. What is Justine's habit of enjoining people to "act simply" if not the overflow of a Jamesian belief that perfect simplicity is perfect goodness?[22] Dudley's gift of his income to the other family members seems initially an unselfish gesture, for instance, but he observes later that most people are slaves of money and that he had to act quickly lest he join their ranks. His withdrawal of the gift upon his engagement to Maria seems a moral betrayal of himself, therefore, and the self-betrayal is complicated in its turn by the reader's suspicion that Maria is marrying him for his money. When Maria is subsequently betrothed to Edgar, the possible understandings are several, but one complex possibility that occurs to the reader is that Edgar anticipates Dudley will reinstate his gifts to the family once he is no longer to be married—that, in effect, Edgar cynically recoups his loss by betraying Dudley and trusting him to be generous in defeat. Dudley complicates *that* possibility with a wholly different level of moral analysis. To the children, who have just realized that Maria will marry Edgar, he says,

I must embarrass you further and tell you that you will have your money back again. I want you to feel some awkwardness which is not caused by my being rejected. No doubt you see that I do. But you will have the money after you have proved that you could give it up. It is just the position one would choose. And I have simply proved that I could take it back. My situation would not be chosen in any way.

The word *simply* is unconsciously ironical in Dudley's speech, for his "simple" morality is intricately reasoned, especially his recognition that the children will enjoy the moral luxury of having behaved selflessly without any lasting surrender of their inevitable self-interest. When he goes on to express himself relieved to surrender the moral *burden* of that luxury, a degree of cynicism is unexpectedly appreciable within his simplicity. Such complications swirl about Dudley's speeches like motes in the middle distance, but Compton-Burnett's greater irony is that Dudley remains entirely credible as the simple, straightforward man whom Justine admires. He thereby mocks the Jamesian innocent who loses his innocence when he learns to be scrupulous, and the reader is effectively brought up short for anticipating more lurid developments than transpire within Dudley's story.

Compton-Burnett was at her mock-Jamesian best in devising such gentle traps for the reader. She was particularly fond of the apparently portentous discussion that seems to go everywhere but really goes nowhere, hedged against irrelevance on the one side because the participants lead narrowly circumscribed lives, hedged against denouement on the other, because their circumscription by the family makes ultimate confrontation impractical. All they can do is joust inconclusively in place. A scene in which Matty joins the family at breakfast on the morning after Blanche's funeral is a fine example of such a scene. The opening thrust is Matty's: "Now, is anyone good and brave enough to say that he has had a good night?" "Brave in what sense?" demands Clement. Seeing immediately her trap but not successfully evading the question's presumption, Mark parries, "I am not going to admit that I have no heart and no feeling." "So you slept well, dear?" she asks sweetly. Justine enters the fray a few minutes later and objects that it is rather soon to ask them to feel better and brighter. "Yes, it is, dear," says Matty, "but I catch a return of spirit in those words, a note of hope and resolve for the future." In her generous way Justine concedes a special status to her aunt's sorrow, but

Matty is too experienced in the lists not to counter the devaluation of her grief:

> "Poor Aunt Matty [says Justine], you are old and helpless and alone, and we give ourselves to our own sorrow and forget your greater need. For your need is greater, *though your sorrow is less.*"
>
> "Yes, that is how *you* would see me, dear. That is how I should *seem* to you all, now that my sister is gone. I must thank you for *trying* to feel kindly towards what you *see.*" [emphasis mine]

Clement laughs at that point, and the jousting *is* funny, for it is mechanically sportive—a game of macabre one-upmanship among both the truly and the falsely grieving. No portentous developments ensue, as they would in a Jamesian scene of comparably sheathed ferocity.

Such arabesques of plotting in *A Family and a Fortune* evoke the lurid formulae of other Compton-Burnett novels. The reader who recalls the psychosexual dynamics of *More Women Than Men* cannot help speculating that homosexual incestuousness underlies the relationship between Dudley and Edgar, especially when Dudley confesses to Maria, "I like Edgar best," and she answers, "He feels the same for you." Yet there is, in fact, no clear indication that the men's liking for one another is in any way erotic, however much they are fond of walking arm in arm and however much the servants may gossip. It will seem to the Compton-Burnett aficionado that Justine's tendency to take over her mother's role is indicative of an Electra complex, and supportive hints are not lacking: Justine habitually calls for admiration of her father and uncle, for instance, and she wafts them secret kisses from across the room. Yet Justine readily surrenders the materfamilias role to Maria when the situation makes it proper, and the last scene in the novel shows her entirely, even triumphantly unchanged as she emits a little cry of pleasure and calls her brothers to admire the sight of Edgar and Dudley walking together.

Such uncharacteristically sunny developments make clear that one of Compton-Burnett's central ploys in *A Family and a Fortune* is to evoke the dark world of Freudian understanding that had earned her a considerable reputation by 1939 and then to pretend she has not evoked it. Set in the year 1901, the novel is resolutely of a period in which Freud had not yet given a prurient interpretation to signs of tenderness among persons of the same sex and among family members of the same and different sexes. The novel belongs to that pre-Freudian period not only in the life and sensibilities it depicts, but, more importantly, in the implied author's lack of sophistication about such things. The implied author simply takes no notice of the Freudian depths while skating insouciantly on their surface. Effectively, she dares the depths to absorb a story that she places in the sunlight. Compton-Burnett, in her turn, affects to know nothing whatsoever about the homoerotic and incestuous aspects of sexuality that are elsewhere her obsession.[23]

The melodramatic staples of Compton-Burnett's plots receive much the same treatment as these Freudian staples. Although she is established as Matty's spy within the house, Maria never functions in that role and is allowed to prove herself good, loving, and wise in that most suspect of late-Victorian roles, the stepmother. An incipient romance between Dudley and Miss Griffin comes to nothing, even though they are cast as kindred orphans in a literal snowstorm. Clement is cast as a miser, yet his miserliness is on a drearily small scale and he harms no one, not even, in any significant way, himself.

As her final vindication suggests, Justine is the most surprising figure in a novel of continual surprises and the most carefully developed. She seems at first a minor character, inasmuch as her officiousness makes her a family joke. "I don't know," she observes in a discussion of whether people should look to others for self-knowledge; "We might often meet a good, sound, impartial judgement." With a livelier sense of alternate possibilities, the family parodies her judiciousness:

> "And we know, when we have one described like that, what a dreadful judgement it is," said her uncle.
> "Half the truth, the blackest of lies," said Mark.
> "The whitest of lies, really," said Clement. "Or there is no such thing as a white lie."
> "Well, there is not," said his sister. "Truth is truth and a lie is a lie."
> "What is Truth?" said Aubrey. "Has Justine told us?"

Certainly the family recognizes a need to restrain Justine's instinct to take charge of things. Blanche is not pleased to find her place usurped as the dispenser of coffee in the morning; Edgar and Dudley find her attentions almost suffocating; and everyone is exasperated by her injunctions to right feeling. When she testifies rhapsodically to Matty's advantages ("You are in your virtual prime; you have health and looks and brains; and we are going to expect a good deal from you"), Blanche asks testily, "My dear, did Aunt Matty ask you to sum up her position?" In fidelity to her high principles, Justine is just as apt to reprove Matty for unkind remarks. On one such occasion, Matty inquires sweetly, "No one is to make a comment but you, dear?" Although he vastly prefers Justine to Matty, Aubrey is quick to comment, "Justine does make them."

Justine is a clownish figure, then, but it is her girl-guide virtues and exaggerated self-assurance that enable her to stand up to Matty, and she manages to keep her footing through it all in a context that invites pratfalls. Although not notably intelligent, she is perceptive in her understandings of people. She recognizes for what they are Clement's meanness of spirit, Aubrey's adolescent insecurity, and Blanche's diffidence about playing a mother's role. She senses almost at once Matty's threat to the family's equilibrium, and she is surprisingly perceptive in her recognition that the close relationship between Edgar and Dudley is somehow basic to the family's emotional balance. Like Matty, Justine is driven by a passion to be needed, but the differences between the two are that Matty is destructive in her drivenness, whereas Justine is entirely constructive; that Matty is egotistical, whereas Justine is carefully self-effacing. Justine's keeping to her chosen course of virtue makes her, in fact, a charmingly woodenheaded heroine in a family threatened by too many changes and by too much cleverness.

Appositely, Brigid Brophy has suggested that Compton-Burnett's technique in all this is that of the *faux naïf* painter, "one who, unable to render either adults or children, depicts both as charmingly wooden dolls."[24] In her absurd tidiness of effect and in her substitution of talking heads for characters, Compton-Burnett might possibly be thought a true naïf—a Grandma Moses of the novel—but she is in actuality no such thing. The complete disclosure of a character's mind is as essential to her art as to the art of *Ulysses,* and the economy of means by which she conveys that mind could not have been more carefully calculated by the author of *The Ambassadors*—no matter that Compton-Burnett substitutes for internal stream of consciousness an external stream in which her characters simply announce every thought that crosses their minds; no matter that she substitutes for the Jamesian *facelle* everyone present at the breakfast table. This is not to say that Compton-

Burnett is the artistic equal of a Joyce or a James but that her carefully considered methods, her self-mockery, and her adroit play with Freudian understandings and melodramatic plots make clear her *faux naïf* posture—a classic posture of the camp artist. Not Grandma Moses, says Brophy: Grandma Oedipus.[25]

8

Again, the Camp Enterprise

It has been suggested repeatedly in these pages that the amorality of camp humor is one of its defining characteristics—that camp is, in effect, a frivolity unbound by conventional considerations of morality. To recognize that camp humorists are as various in temperament and technique as are Peacock, Beerbohm, Firbank, Benson, Wodehouse, and Compton-Burnett is to recognize that camp is a frivolity unbound by a tradition as well. One can speak of a tradition of camping in the English novel, of course, pointing to strands of influence that connect Fielding's *Jonathan Wild* with *Headlong Hall* and the dialogic technique of Firbank with that of Compton-Burnett, but such strands of influence are largely happenstantial. They do not constitute a tradition in the sense of designating an essential line of development, distinguished from the accidental and the peripheral. Certainly the six novelists featured in these pages had no sense of writing within such a tradition.

Rather than as a distinct genre or as one strand of a tradition braided with other strands into something like F. R. Leavis's Great Tradition, it seems more reasonable today to think of camp as an occasional, sometimes fortuitously discovered thread in the fabric of literature—the intermittent warp to a woof provided by such conventional genres as satire (*Headlong Hall*), romantic fantasy (*Zuleika Dobson*), hagiography (*The Flower beneath the Foot*), the novel of manners (*Mapp and Lucia*), farce (*Right Ho, Jeeves*), Freudian melodrama (*More Women Than Men*), and any number of other genres. Indeed, the propensity of literary camp for interweaving itself with the canonically approved genres seems a natural, perhaps inevitable, strategy for accommodating its special audacity. Artifice, stylization, and exaggeration find useful some bounded standard by which to manifest themselves unbounded, and the canonical genres serve them in that function much in the way that gender stereotypes served Garbo's camp androgyny and in the way that the deadpan banality of the duke and duchess of Windsor made camp their celebrity status.

Haunting the concept of a camp tradition is the problem of intention. With the exception of Firbank, who knew he was camping, it is doubtful that the novelists discussed in these pages would happily hear themselves described as camps, and not only because they would have found today's use of the term unfamiliar. Compton-Burnett thought of herself as a serious novelist; Peacock, as a topical satirist; Beerbohm, Benson, and Wodehouse as workaday light novelists. If their status as camps is contingent upon a style of apprehension and appreciation more resonant today than in their historical moments, it is not, for reason of that temporal limitation, invalid. Arguably, all modes of aesthetic and rhetorical appreciation have their origin in temporal sensibilities, and the application of latter-day modalities of thought to primitive, classical, and even neoclassical literatures is a greatly traveled road. The sensibility has, in the last analysis, its imperatives. The architects of St. Mark's Square in Venice were serious-minded men, not camps, but who can view their incomparable piazza today without delighting to at least some degree in its campiness? Who is not charmed—*dis*armed, really—by Reginald Hill's description of the piazza as "absurd, impossible, and beautiful beyond comprehension, as if Michelangelo, Christopher Wren, Walt Disney, and God had sat in committee to build it"?[1] The camp vision is not only amoral and ahistorical, it would seem; it is also a-rational, and Hill pays tribute to the extraordinary dynamics of the piazza by inviting us to disarm our reason.

All humor might be considered a technique of psychological disarmament, of course. If one considers the extremes to which human disapproval can resort, laughter is notably gentle in its critiques and disarms its subjects by defining all possibility of a violent response as de trop. In effect, humor pretends to walk unarmed in order to disarm its subjects of retaliatory righteousness. But camp genuinely disarms itself of humor's most potent weapons: morality and right reason. Frivolously, it chooses to love in a manner amoral, ahistorical, and a-rational all that is both exaggerated in style and negligible in content—which is to say that it chooses unboundedly, in a spirit of frivolity, to love frivolity itself. The integrity of camp's unorthodox enterprise is perhaps not arguable, but it is clearly phenomenal.

Notes

Chapter 1: The Camp Enterprise

1. Edith Wharton, *A Backward Glance* (New York: Appleton-Century, 1934), pp. 242–43.

2. J. Redding Ware, *Passing English of the Victorian Era* (New York: Dutton, 1909), p. 61. The French word Ware had in mind is not clear. Partridge suggests an alternate possibility that the word evolved from a nineteenth-century dialectical use of *camp* or *kemp* (meaning "uncouth" or "rough") that came to mean "slightly disreputable" or "bogus." Eric Partridge, *A Dictionary of Slang and Unconventional English,* 8th ed. (London: Routledge and Kegan Paul, 1984), p. 176.

3. For a brief analysis of the word's history as an adjective, see William White, "'Camp' as Adjective: 1909–66," *American Speech* 41 (1966): 70–72. For a tangentially related discussion of the onomastics of camp, see Leonard R. N. Ashley, "'Lovely, Blooming, Fresh, and Gay': The Onomastics of Camp," *Maledicta* 4 (Winter 1980): 223–48.

4. Christopher Isherwood, *The World in the Evening* (New York: Farrar, Straus and Giroux, 1954), p. 110. For a related discussion see also Peter Thomas, "'Camp' and Politics in Isherwood's Berlin Fiction," *Journal of Modern Literature* 5 (February 1976): 117–30.

5. Ibid., p. 110.

6. Susan Sontag, "Notes on 'Camp,'" *Against Interpretation* (New York: Dell, 1969), p. 280. The essay was originally published in *Partisan Review* (Fall 1964): 515–30. For an important but ineffective attack on Sontag's essay, see Louis D. Rubin, Jr., "Susan Sontag and the Camp Followers," *Sewanee Review* 82 (Summer 1974): 503–10.

7. Ibid., p. 283. Paul Rudnick and Kurt Anderson have recently refocused Sontag's 1964 distinction into a 1989 distinction between real camp (which they see as ironic) and "camp lite" (by which term they designate a nonintellectual, only speciously ironic celebration of artifacts from the supposedly good-old-days). "The Irony Epidemic: How Camp Changed from Lush to Lite," *Spy* (March 1989): 93–98.

8. Ibid.
9. *The Random House Dictionary of the English Language,* unabridged edition, sv *camp.*
10. *The Random House Dictionary of the English Language,* 2nd edition, unabridged, sv *camp.*
11. Sontag, p. 282.
12. Esther Newton, *Mother Camp: Female Impersonators in America* (Chicago: University of Chicago Press, 1979), p. 105.
13. Ibid., p. 106.
14. Parker Tyler, "The Garbo Image," *The Films of Greta Garbo,* ed. Michael Conroy, Dion McGregor, and Mark Ricci (New York: Citadel, n.d.), p. 28.
15. E. F. Benson, *Final Edition* (New York: Appleton-Century, 1940), p. 77.
16. Ibid., p. 171.
17. Sontag, p. 278.
18. Elizabeth Bowen, Review of *Elders and Betters* by Ivy Compton-Burnett. Reprinted in *The Art of I. Compton-Burnett: A Collection of Critical Essays,* ed. Charles Burkhart (London: Gollancz, 1972), p. 58.

Chapter 2: Thomas Love Peacock

1. J. B. Priestley, *Thomas Love Peacock,* introduction by J. I. M. Stewart (New York: St. Martin's, 1966), p. 195.
2. The seminal text arguing this position is Jean-Jacques Mayoux's *Un Epicurien Anglais* (Paris: Presses Modernes, 1932). See also Marilyn Butler, *Peacock Displayed: A Satirist in His Context* (London: Routledge and Kegan Paul, 1979). Butler places Peacock's satire in a context of the social unrest following the Napoleonic Wars and the campaign for political reform around 1830.
3. Priestley, p. 101.
4. See especially Peacock's remarks on Old Comedy in his review of C. O. Müller and J. W. Donaldson's *History of Greek Literature, Fraser's* (March 1859). Reprinted in the *Halliford Edition of the Works of Thomas Love Peacock,* ed. H. F. B. Brett-Smith and C. E. James, 10 vols. (New York: AMS, 1967), 10:201.

5. A well-argued case for this view of Peacock as an entertainer is developed by A. E. Dyson, "Peacock: The Wand of Enchantment," *The Crazy Fabric* (London: Macmillan, 1965), pp. 57–71.

6. I am not the first to make this point. David Garnett calls the characters "mouthpieces of ideas" rather than faithful portraits of men. *The Novels of Thomas Love Peacock,* 2 vols. (London: Hart-Davis, 1948), 1:8.

7. Priestley, p. 107. Priestley apparently borrowed the notion of Peacock as a court jester from a nineteenth-century review by James Spedding, "Tales by the Author of Headlong Hall," *Edinburgh Review* 68 (January 1839). Or he was perhaps inspired by Peacock's own description of Rabelais as "one of the wisest and most learned, as well as the wittiest of men, [who] put on the role of the all-licensed fool, that he might, like the court-jester, convey bitter truths under the semblance of simple buffoonery." "French Comic Romances," *Works,* 9:258–59.

8. Letter from Peacock to Shelley dated 15 September 1818, *Works,* 8:204.

9. Letter from Peacock to Shelley dated 30 May 1818, *Works,* 8:193.

10. The second I have discussed in this chapter but the third in a Pavonine novel. Mr. Moly Mystic in *Melincourt* and Mr. Skionar in *Crotchet Castle* are also caricatures.

11. Bryan Burns points out that the character Scythrop was not formally linked to Shelley until long after the book was published and that neither Peacock's own letters nor those of his friends ever mention the link. *The Novels of Thomas Love Peacock* (Totowa, NJ: Barnes and Noble Books, 1985), p. 88.

12. Letter 21 dated 20/21 (?) June 1819 in *Peacock's Memoirs of Shelley with Shelley's Letters to Peacock,* ed. H. F. B. Brett-Smith (London: Henry Frowde, 1909), p. 190.

13. Edmund Burke, *A Philosophical Enquiry into the Origin of Our Ideas of the Sublime and Beautiful,* ed. J. T. Boulton (London: Routledge and Kegan Paul, 1985), p. 149. Robert Kiely seems to have been the first to identify the parody of Burke in *The Romantic Novel in England* (Cambridge: Harvard University Press, 1972), p. 14.

14. Which is not to say that it disappeared from more libidinous repositories of English humor than the nineteenth-century novel, which was committed to cross-breeding with educational and moral treatises. It clearly survived in the libretti of W. S. Gilbert, for instance; it survived as well within homosexual coteries and their more-or-less

private entertainments in the universities. The occasional crocheteer in Dickens and passage in Bulwer-Lytton might possibly be understood as camp, but in their larger structures of meaning Dickens's and Bulwer-Lytton's novels militate against such understandings. *Alice in Wonderland,* I submit, is sui generis—not a novel.

Chapter 3: Max Beerbohm

1. E. M. Forster, *Aspects of the Novel* (New York: Harcourt, Brace, 1927), p. 118.
2. Max Beerbohm, *Zuleika Dobson; or, An Oxford Love Story* (New York: Dodd, Mead, 1946), np.
3. Louis Kronenberger, "The Perfect Trifler," *Saturday Review of Literature* (21 June 1947): 42.
4. Edmund Wilson, "Analysis of Max Beerbohm," *New Yorker* (1 May 1948): 96.
5. Guy Boas records the moment in "The Magic of Max," *Blackwood's Magazine* 260 (November 1946): 341.
6. F. W. Dupee chronicles the remark in "Beerbohm: The Rigors of Fantasy," *New York Review of Books* (9 June 1966): 17.
7. S. N. Behrman, *Portrait of Max: An Intimate Memoir of Sir Max Beerbohm* (New York: Random House, 1960), p. 258. Behrman interested himself for several years in writing a stage version of *Zuleika Dobson;* thus, his examination of the manuscripts. For a detailed study of the manuscripts, see Robert Viscusi, *Max Beerbohm; or, the Dandy Dante: Rereading with Mirrors* (Baltimore: Johns Hopkins, 1986), pp. 133–47.
8. The exact year of Zuleika's adventures is generally calculated as 1905, but see Harold Nicholson on the problem of contradictory textual evidence vis-à-vis the date. "*Zuleika Dobson*—a Revaluation," *The Listener,* 25 (September 1947): 521–22. Judas College is, of course, an invention.
9. Where her adventures continued in a novel by Sydney Roberts called *Zuleika in Cambridge* (London: Heffer, 1941). Beerbohm himself resuscitated Zuleika in a letter she addressed to the composer George Gershwin, who was thinking of turning her story into a stage musical. She censures Beerbohm's version of her life in that letter and adds an interesting postscript: "I was married, secretly, to the late Lord Kitchener, early in 1915. Being so worried by his great responsibilities at that time, he no longer had the grit to cope with my importunities,

poor fellow." The letter is quoted in full by David Cecil in *Max: A Biography* (Cambridge: Houghton Mifflin, 1964), pp. 372–73.

10. Matthew Arnold, preface to *Essays in Criticism: First Series* (London: Macmillan, 1932), p. xi.

11. Dupee, 13.

12. *The Works of Max Beerbohm* with a bibliography by John Lane (London: John Lane, The Bodley Head, 1986). In a kindred joke, Beerbohm gave place on his bookshelves in Rapallo to an excessively thin volume he had fabricated and entitled "The Complete Works of Arnold Bennett." Bennett's prodigious output he always affected to find amazing.

13. It should perhaps be said that there is no real model for the Zuleika Dobson "well known . . . to all of you by repute." Insofar as there is a model at all, it seems to have been a fifteen-year-old music hall singer named Cissie Loftus, with whom Beerbohm was briefly infatuated while he was a student at Oxford. See *Max Beerbohm: Letters to Reggie Turner,* ed. Rupert Hart-Davis (London: Ambassador, 1964), pp. 53, 72.

Chapter 4: Ronald Firbank

1. Cyril Connolly, "The Novel-Addict's Cupboard," *The Condemned Playground, Essays: 1927–1944* (New York: Macmillan, 1946), p. 115.

2. E. M. Forster, "Ronald Firbank," *Abinger Harvest* (New York: Harcourt, Brace, 1936), p. 115.

3. Not unrecognized by Brigid Brophy, whose critical biography of Firbank argues precisely these points, but in so partisan a way that the point has not generally been taken. Brophy, *Prancing Novelist: A Defence of Fiction in the Form of a Critical Biography in Praise of Ronald Firbank* (New York: Harper and Row, 1973).

4. Evelyn Waugh, "Ronald Firbank," *The Essays, Articles and Reviews of Evelyn Waugh,* ed. Donat Gallagher (Boston: Little, Brown, 1984), p. 56.

5. Brophy, p. 100.

6. Ibid., p. 171.

7. Firbank summarized the place in the phrase "some imaginary Vienna," having discovered his imaginary Vienna while in the Sahara—which circumstance possibly explains the improbable aura of Pisuerga.

Author's preface to the first American edition of *The Flower Beneath the Foot* (New York: Brentano's, 1924), np.

8. Because Firbank used rice powder and other cosmetics, Brophy suggests that the Arabian mare is an auctorial self-portrait. Brophy, *Prancing Novelist,* p. 154.

9. It must be remarked at this early point that Firbank's novels enshrine many unorthodoxies of spelling and grammar, as *naughtyness* here. Indeed, the opening sentence of *Flower Beneath the Foot* is ungrammatical, and the opening sentence of the American preface contains a spelling mistake. Malapropisms also abound. Brophy suggests that Firbank's defiance of linguistic orthodoxy is at its most outrageous in *Flower Beneath the Foot* "because that book is his highest protest against the rules of English behavior." Ibid., p. 523.

10. Portraits of Victoria Sackville-West ("Mrs. Chillywater") and Evan Morgan ("Eddie Montieth") are perhaps exceptions to this point, but I would argue that the portraits in their published form stop short of satiric caricature. In the original manuscript sent to the publisher Grant Richard, Eddie Montieth's name was "Heaven Organ," apparent revenge for Firbank's onetime lover having refused the dedication of *The Princess Zubaroff* and insisting that it be excised from the already-bound volumes. Richard demanded Firbank change the suggestive "Heaven Organ" lest the novel provoke a libel suit from Morgan. For further discussion of these matters, see Miriam J. Benkovitz, "More about Ronald Firbank," *Columbia Library Columns* 26, 2 (1977): 3–12.

11. For commercial reasons, Carl Van Vechten wanted the title "Prancing Nigger" for the first American edition, and the title has become standard, although Firbank preferred "Sorrow in Sunlight" and insisted upon its use in the first English edition.

12. It must be remarked that Firbank was not a racist and, in fact, identified with blacks. For an interesting consideration of the topic, see Brophy, pp. 173–76, 202–4.

13. Kenneth Burke, "Dictionary of Pivotal Terms," *Attitudes toward History* (Boston: Beacon, 1961), pp. 308–14.

14. For a further diagnosis of the Firbankian world with emphases not my own, see Robert Murray Davis, "'Hyperaesthesia with Complications': The World of Ronald Firbank," *Rendezvous* 3, 1 (1968): 5–15.

15. Brophy, p. 552.

16. The letter in which Brentano's declined to publish the novel is cited in Miriam J. Benkovitz, *A Bibliography of Ronald Firbank* (London: Hart-Davis, 1963), p. 50.

17. Brophy argues that "The great scarlet splurge of his Cardinal is the most tragic and the fullest of Firbank's self-portraits, and it is a portrait of Firbank in [Oscar] Wilde's tragic robes. Pirelli is Wilde unidealized by prudence, the Wilde who went to judgment (on his eccentricity) and to death." Brophy, p. 564.

18. Edward Martin Potoker has observed, "though [Firbank's] writing is often concerned with evil, it is naughtiness that he really portrays. All behavior, particularly sexual behavior, is fun." *Ronald Firbank* (New York: Columbia University Press, 1969), p. 12. W. H. Auden once remarked, "The improprieties in Firbank are those of children playing Doctor behind the rhododendron bushes." His sexual acts, says Auden, are "infantile and polymorphously perverse." "Ronald Firbank and an Amateur World," *The Listener* (8 June 1961): 1004–5.

19. Cited in Benkovitz, *A Bibliography of Ronald Firbank*, p. 50.

Chapter 5: E. F. Benson

1. The bibliographical count is by Cynthia and Tony Reavell, *E. F. Benson: Mr. Benson Remembered in Rye, and the World of Tilling* (Rye, England: Martello Bookshop, 1984), pp. 2–5.

2. E. F. Benson, *Final Edition* (New York: Appleton-Century, 1940), p. 191.

3. Ibid., p. 260.

4. E. F. Benson, *Make Way for Lucia* (including the novels *Queen Lucia, Lucia in London, Miss Mapp, Mapp and Lucia, The Worshipful Lucia, Trouble for Lucia,* and a short story "The Male Impersonator") introduced by Nancy Mitford (New York: Harper and Row, 1986). This is a reissue of an omnibus originally published in 1977 by Thomas Y. Crowell Company.

5. Peppino became "Pepino" in later novels, but the spelling has been standardized in the omnibus *Make Way for Lucia,* whose lead I follow both in this standardization and in the standardization of American spellings in the Mapp and Lucia texts.

6. Riseholme is based primarily upon Broadway in the Cotswolds, but Stratford-upon-Avon enters the picture inasmuch as Lucia is based partly upon the popular novelist Marie Corelli, who was both a patron and an inhabitant of Stratford-upon-Avon. Cynthia and Tony Reavell point out that when the novels were first published Lucia was widely believed to have been based on Lady Sybil Colefax. In Rye it was thought Lucia owed something to Mrs. Dacre Vincent (Margaret), who dominated musical life in the town. Reavell, pp. 90–91.

7. Benson, *Final Edition,* pp. 171–72.

8. Such phrases recur in novels outside the Mapp and Lucia sequence, too; Benson did not hesitate to reemploy a good line or character. Miss Howard in *Paying Guests* echoes Lucia, for instance, in exclaiming, "How you all work me!" when she is affecting a mood of abstraction over the piano keys.

9. Mapp is referred to as "Elizabeth" in the novels after her marriage to Major Benjy. Not to confuse the reader, I refer to her consistently as "Mapp."

10. V. S. Pritchett, "E. F. Benson: Fairy Tales," *The Tale Bearers: Literary Essays* (New York: Random House, 1980), p. 23.

11. A female mayor with an officially designated mayoress carries to an absurdity the actual custom of bachelor mayors appointing official mayoresses. Himself mayor of Rye from 1934 through 1937, Benson was served by Mrs. Reta Jacomb-Hood in that capacity, conjoined with her in what he liked to call "municipal sin."

12. Nancy Mitford makes a pertinent comment: "I was a fellow guest at Highcliffe, with Mr. E. F. Benson soon after Lucia had become Mayor of Tilling. We talked of her for hours and he said, 'What must she do now?' Alas, he died in the first year of the war; can we doubt that if he had lived Lucia would have become a General?" Introduction to E. F. Benson, *Make Way for Lucia,* p. x. But Mitford's speculation has been outdated by the novelist Tom Holt, who has given Luciaphils two (at this writing) fine novels based on Benson's characters: *Lucia in Wartime* (1985) and *Lucia Triumphant* (1986). In the first, Lucia does not quite snare a generalship, but to the awe of Tilling she does manage to make Mallards available for a secret meeting of Churchill, Eisenhower, and De Gaulle.

13. Susan Sontag, "Notes on 'Camp,'" *Against Interpretation* (New York: Dell, 1969), p. 281.

Chapter 6: P. G. Wodehouse

1. The standard bibliography is David A. Jasen, *A Bibliography and Reader's Guide to the First Editions of P. G. Wodehouse* (Hamden, CT: Archon Books, 1970). See also J. F. Whitt, *The Strand Magazine 1891–1950: A Selective Checklist Listing All Material Relating to Arthur Conan Doyle, All Stories by P. G. Wodehouse, and a Selection of Other Contributors* (London: J. F. Whitt, 1979).

2. *Daily Telegraph,* 8 July 1941.
3. George Orwell, "In Defense of P. G. Wodehouse," *The Collected Essays, Journalism and Letters of George Orwell,* 4 vols., ed. Sonia Orwell and Ian Angus (New York: Harcourt, Brace and World, 1968), 3:351.
4. See, for instance, Wodehouse to W. T. Townen: "With world convulsions happening every hour upon the hour, I appear to be still the rather backward lad I was when we brewed our first cup of tea in our study together." Quoted in P. G. Wodehouse, *Performing Flea* (London: Herbert Jenkins, 1953), p. 214.
5. P. G. Wodehouse, *Performing Flea,* published in America as *Author! Author!* (New York: Simon and Schuster, 1962). The volume is not really the collection of original letters that it appears to be but an autobiographical reminiscence. The letters have been elaborately revised.
6. Hilaire Belloc in a broadcast to America during the 1930s, cited in Frances Donaldson, *P. G. Wodehouse: A Biography* (London: Weidenfeld and Nicholson, 1982), p. 1. In 1939 Belloc amplified his remarks in his introduction to *Weekend Wodehouse* (London: Herbert Jenkins, 1939).
7. Auberon Waugh, "Father of the English Idea," *Homage to P. G. Wodehouse,* ed. Thelma Cazalet-Keir (London: Barrie and Jenkins, 1973), p. 144.
8. Both blurbs are cited in more permanent form in an advertising appendix to the first edition of *Right Ho, Jeeves* (London: Herbert Jenkins, 1934), np.
9. "Publisher's Salute," *New York Times,* 14 October 1960, p. 31. Wodehouse had to explain to the American publishers Simon and Schuster, who sponsored the two-column salutation in conjunction with their publication of *The Most of P. G. Wodehouse,* that they had mistaken the year of his birth. Instead of a proper eightieth-birthday salute, therefore, the salutation greets Wodehouse on entering his eightieth year.
10. Bertie appears as early as 1916 in a story called "Extricating Young Gussie," in which his surname is apparently not "Wooster" but "Mannering-Phipps." Jeeves is at that point an obscure servant.
11. In a 1944 letter to Denis Mackail, Wodehouse observed, "The actual writing of a story always give me a guilty feeling, as if I were wasting

my time. The only thing that matters is thinking the stuff out." Quoted in Donaldson, 30.

12. Robert A. Hall, Jr., *The Comic Style of P. G. Wodehouse* (Hamden, CT: Archon Books, 1974), p. 23.

13. Donaldson, p. 15.

14. Richard Usborne, *Wodehouse at Work to the End* (London: Barrie and Jenkins, 1976), p. 175.

15. The entanglement of Wodehouse's characters always complicates plots sufficiently complex in themselves. Although *Joy in the Morning* does not allude to the fact, devotees of the short stories will recall that Jeeves mentions in "Jeeves Takes Charge" that he was once Lord Worplesdon's valet for about a year. Thus, Worplesdon's knowledge of Jeeves's consulting practice.

16. Richard Usborne suggests it is the very best of all. Usborne, *Wodehouse at Work,* p. 18. But see Donaldson, p. 29, for a dissenting opinion.

17. I am consciously echoing Jessica Milner Davis's fine translation of a passage from Henri Bergson's monograph *Le Rire:* "The vaudevilliste's art probably lies in presenting us with an arrangement of human events whose interior clockwork is evident, while at the same time it preserves an external appearance of probability, that is, of the apparent suppleness of life." *Farce* (London: Methuen, 1978), p. 61.

18. Richard Usborne, *A Wodehouse Companion* (London: Hamish Hamilton, 1981), p. 69.

19. Donaldson, pp. 54, 126.

20. David Jasen, *P. G. Wodehouse: A Portrait of a Master* (London: Garnstone, 1975), p. 3.

21. Cited in Donaldson, p. 11.

22. A. P. Ryan, "Wooster's Progress," *New Statesman and Nation* (20 June 1953): 737.

23. Both Donaldson and R. B. D. French have argued persuasively against the assumption that Wodehouse was serious in his depiction of aunts. Donaldson, pp. 10–12; French, *P. G. Wodehouse* (London: Oliver and Boyd, 1966), p. 57.

24. See French, p. 102, for a complementary discussion of Jeeves being foil to his master, not vice versa.

25. See n. 3, above.

26. Claud Cockburn, "Wodehouse All the Way," *Homage to P. G. Wodehouse,* p. 42.

Chapter 7: Ivy Compton-Burnett

1. See, for instance, A. Norman Jeffares, speech of introduction to the awarding of the doctor of letters degree, Leeds University, 19 May 1960, *The Art of I. Compton-Burnett: A Collection of Critical Essays,* ed. Charles Burkhart (London: Gollancz, 1972), p. 17; Robert Liddell, "The Novels of I. Compton-Burnett," *A Treatise on the Novel* (London: Jonathan Cape, 1947), pp. 146–47; Charles Burkhart, ed., introduction to *The Art of I. Compton-Burnett: A Collection of Critical Essays,* p. 8.

2. See, for instance, Anthony Powell, obituary notice for Ivy Compton-Burnett, *Spectator* (6 September 1969): 304.

3. See, for instance, John Ginger, "Ivy Compton-Burnett," *London Magazine* (January 1970): 65.

4. M. Jourdain, "I. Compton-Burnett and M. Jourdain: A Conversation," *Orion, A Miscellany* 1 (London: Nicholson and Watson, 1945), p. 25.

5. Elizabeth Bowen, review of *Parents and Children* by Ivy Compton-Burnett. Reprinted in *Collected Impressions* (New York: Knopf, 1950), p. 84.

6. Raymond Mortimer, review of *A House and Its Head* by I. Compton-Burnett, *New Statesman and Nation* (13 July 1935): 66.

7. Edward Sackville-West, "Ladies Whose Bright Pens . . . ," *Inclinations* (London: Secker and Warburg, 1949), p. 86.

8. Charles Burkhart, "Compton-Burnett: The Shape of a Career," *The Art of I. Compton-Burnett,* pp. 104–5.

9. Powell, p. 304.

10. Nathalie Sarraute, "Conversation and Sub-Conversation," *The Age of Suspicion,* trans. Maria Jolas (New York: Braziller, 1963), pp. 75–117.

11. Jourdain, p. 21.

12. The photograph is reproduced in Hilary Spurling, *Ivy: The Life of I. Compton-Burnett* (New York: Knopf, 1984), facing page 430.

13. Compton-Burnett's technical knowledge of homosexuals and their distinction from transvestites, bisexuals, and other types does not seem

to have been extensive. Because she associates all such types with the homosexual inclination, I have associated them in interpreting her position.

14. Sarraute, p. 114.
15. Quoted by Mario Praz, "The Novels of Ivy Compton-Burnett," RAI Radio (Televisione Italiana), 1 April 1955.
16. Pamela Hansford Johnson, *I. Compton-Burnett* (London: British Council/Longmans, 1951), p. 42.
17. No psychological sophistication is required to discern the source of such motifs in Compton-Burnett's status as the eldest child of her father's second marriage, in her father's sudden death when she was sixteen, and in the family's financial difficulties thereafter. She knew what it was to be an aspiring novelist who was the daughter of a popular writer, and like Frances Ponsonby she kept secret from her family her first submission to a publisher. The plight of governesses she had witnessed in the Compton-Burnett nursery, and in a family of fourteen the murmured aside was her habit as much as it is that of the Ponsonby children.
18. See n. 15, above.
19. In her personal copy of Butler's *Note-Books,* Compton-Burnett scored heavy lines beside a passage that must have seemed to her an exoneration of her thoroughly unsentimental view of family dynamics:

    The Family

    I believe that more unhappiness comes from this source than from any other—I mean from the attempt to prolong family connection unduly and to make people hang together artificially who would never naturally do so. The mischief among the lower classes is not so great, but among the middle and upper classes it is killing a large number daily. And the old people do not really like it much better than the young.

    The Note-Books of Samuel Butler, ed. Henry Festing Jones (London: Fifield, 1912), p. 31. Compton-Burnett's copy of the *Note-Books,* with her annotations, is among the Marsden-Smedley papers, miscellaneous documents that once belonged to Ivy Compton-Burnett and Margaret Jourdain, inherited by Hester Marden-Smedley, and now in the possession of her daughter, Henrietta Williamson.
20. Published originally in America under the title *Bullivant and the Lambs.*
21. Angus Wilson goes so far as to name it first among the author's masterpieces. Obituary of Ivy Compton-Burnett, *Observer* (31 August

1960). Reprinted in *The Art of I. Compton-Burnett: A Collection of Critical Essays,* p. 193.

22. Hilary Spurling observes that Compton-Burnett invariably deprecated James's achievement and repeatedly denied his influence. "I hate people whose golden bowls are broken," says Lady Hardistry in *Men and Wives.* Spurling, p. 147.

23. The apparent suicide pact consummated in 1917 by Compton-Burnett's younger sisters, Katherine and Stephanie, was rumored in later years to have been a result of their allegedly lesbian relationship. Compton-Burnett ignored the rumors, just as she ignored (without quite discouraging) most of the rumors that circulated about herself. Just so, in *A Family and a Fortune,* she ignores without quite discouraging the possibility that a significant number of her characters are caught up in homoerotic and/or incestuous relationships.

24. Brigid Brophy, review of *A God and His Gifts* by Ivy Compton-Burnett, *New Statesman* (December 1963). Reprinted in Brigid Brophy, *Don't Never Forget: Collected Views and Reviews* (New York: Holt, Rinehart and Winston, 1967), p. 170.

25. Brophy, *Don't Never Forget,* p. 170.

Chapter 8: Again, the Camp Enterprise

1. Reginald Hill, *Another Death in Venice* (New York: New American Library, 1987), p. 118.

Bibliography of Works Cited

Primary Texts

Beerbohm, Max. *Max Beerbohm: Letters to Reggie Turner.* Edited by Rupert Hart-Davis. London: Ambassador, 1964.

———. *The Works of Max Beerbohm.* Bibliography by John Lane. London: John Lane, The Bodley Head, 1896.

———. *Zuleika Dobson; or, An Oxford Love Story.* New York: Dodd, Mead, 1946.

Benson, E. F. *Final Edition.* New York: Appleton-Century, 1940.

———. *Make Way for Lucia* (omnibus edition including the novels *Queen Lucia, Lucia in London, Miss Mapp, Mapp and Lucia, The Worshipful Lucia, Trouble for Lucia,* and a short story "The Male Impersonator"). Introduction by Nancy Mitford. New York: Crowell, 1977; New York: Harper and Row, 1986.

———. *Paying Guests.* London: Hutchinson, 1929.

Burke, Edmund. *A Philosophical Enquiry into the Origin of Our Ideas of the Sublime and Beautiful.* Edited by J. T. Boulton. London: Routledge and Kegan Paul, 1958.

Butler, Samuel. *The Note-Books of Samuel Butler.* Edited by Henry Festing Jones. London: Fifield, 1912.

Compton-Burnett, Ivy. *Daughters and Sons.* London: Gollancz, 1937.

———. *A Family and a Fortune.* London: Gollancz, 1939.

———. *More Women Than Men.* London: Heinemann, 1933.

Firbank, Ronald. Author's preface, *The Flower Beneath the Foot.* New York: Brentano's, 1924.

———. *The Complete Ronald Firbank* (omnibus edition including *Odette, The Artificial Princess, Vainglory, Inclinations, Caprice, Valmouth, Santal, The Flower Beneath the Foot, Prancing Nigger, Concerning the Eccentricities of Cardinal Pirelli,* and *The Princess Zoubaroff*). Preface by Anthony Powell. London: Duckworth, 1961.

Hill, Reginald. *Another Death in Venice.* New York: New American Library, 1987.

Holt, Tom. *Lucia in Wartime.* London: Macmillan, 1985.

———. *Lucia Triumphant*. London: Macmillan, 1986.
Isherwood, Christopher. *The World in the Evening*. New York: Farrar, Straus, and Giroux, 1954.
Peacock, Thomas Love. *Halliford Edition of the Works of Thomas Love Peacock*. Edited by H. F. B. Brett-Smith and C. E. James. 10 vols. New York: AMS, 1967.
———. *The Novels of Thomas Love Peacock*. Edited by David Garnett. 2 vols. London: Hart-Davis, 1948.
Roberts, Sydney. *Zuleika in Cambridge*. London: Heffer, 1941.
Shelley, Percy Bysshe. *Peacock's Memoirs of Shelley with Shelley's Letters to Peacock*. Edited by H. F. B. Brett-Smith. London: Frowde, 1909.
Wharton, Edith. *A Backward Glance*. New York: Appleton-Century, 1934.
Wodehouse, P. G. *Bertie Wooster Sees It Through*. Published in England as *Jeeves and the Feudal Spirit*. London: Jenkins, 1954.
———. *Joy in the Morning*. London: Jenkins, 1946.
———. *The Mating Season*. London: Jenkins, 1949.
———. *Performing Flea*. London: Jenkins, 1953.
———. *Right Ho, Jeeves*. London: Jenkins, 1934.

Secondary Texts

Arnold, Matthew. *Essays in Criticism: First Series*. London: Macmillan, 1932.
Ashley, Leonard R. N. "'Lovely, Blooming, Fresh and Gay': The Onomastics of Camp." *Maledicta: The International Journal of Verbal Aggression* 4 (Winter 1980): 223–48.
Auden, W. H. "Ronald Firbank and an Amateur World." *The Listener* (8 June 1961): 1004–5, 1008.
Behrman, S. N. *Portrait of Max: An Intimate Memoir of Sir Max Beerbohm*. New York: Random House, 1960.
Belloc, Hilaire. Introduction to *The Weekend Wodehouse*. London: Jenkins, 1939.
Benkovitz, Miriam J. *A Bibliography of Ronald Firbank*. London: Hart-Davis, 1963.
———. "More about Ronald Firbank." *Columbia Library Columns* 26 (1977): 3–12.
Boas, Guy. "The Magic of Max." *Blackwood's Magazine* 260 (November 1946): 341–50. Reprint, Riewald.
Bowen, Elizabeth. Review of *Elders and Betters* by Ivy Compton-Burnett. *Cornhill Magazine*, 1944. Reprint, Burkhart.
———. Review of *Parents and Children* by Ivy Compton-Burnett. *New Statesman and Nation*, 1941. Reprint, *Collected Impressions*. New York: Knopf, 1950. Reprint, Burkhart.

Brophy, Brigid. *Don't Never Forget: Collected Views and Reviews.* New York: Holt, Rinehart and Winston, 1967.

———. *Prancing Novelist: A Defence of Fiction in the Form of a Critical Biography in Praise of Ronald Firbank.* New York: Harper and Row, 1973.

Burke, Kenneth. *Attitudes toward History.* Boston: Beacon, 1961.

Burkhart, Charles, ed. *The Art of I. Compton-Burnett: A Collection of Critical Essays.* London: Gollancz, 1972.

Burns, Bryan. *The Novels of Thomas Love Peacock.* Totowa, NJ: Barnes and Noble, 1985.

Butler, Marilyn. *Peacock Displayed: A Satirist in His Context.* London: Routledge and Kegan Paul, 1979.

Cazalet-Keir, Thelma, ed. *Homage to P. G. Wodehouse.* London: Barrie and Jenkins, 1973.

Cecil, David. *Max: A Biography.* Cambridge: Houghton Mifflin, 1964.

Cockburn, Claud. "Wodehouse All the Way," *Homage to P. G. Wodehouse.* Edited by Thelma Cazalet-Keir. London: Barrie and Jenkins, 1973.

Connolly, Cyril. *The Condemned Playground, Essays: 1927–1944.* New York: Macmillan, 1946.

Conway, Michael, Dion McGregor, and Mark Ricci, eds. *The Films of Greta Garbo.* New York: Citadel Press, nd.

Davis, Jessica Milner. *Farce.* London: Methuen, 1978.

Davis, Robert Murray. "'Hyperaesthesia with Complications': The World of Ronald Firbank." *Rendezvous* 3 (1968): 5–15.

Donaldson, Frances. *P. G. Wodehouse: A Biography.* London: Weidenfeld and Nicholson, 1982.

Dupee, F. W. "Beerbohm: The Rigors of Fantasy." *New York Review of Books* (9 June 1966): 12–17. Reprint, in slightly changed and enlarged form, as "Max Beerbohm and the Rigors of Fantasy" in Riewald.

Dyson, A. E. *The Crazy Fabric.* London: Macmillan, 1965.

Forster, E. M. *Abinger Harvest.* New York: Harcourt, Brace, 1936.

———. *Aspects of the Novel.* New York: Harcourt, Brace, 1927.

French, R. B. D. *P. G. Wodehouse.* London: Oliver and Boyd, 1966.

Ginger, John. "Ivy Compton-Burnett." *London Magazine,* January 1970. Reprint, Burkhart.

Hall, Robert A., Jr. *The Comic Style of P. G. Wodehouse.* Hamden, CT: Archon Books, 1974.

Jasen, David A. *A Bibliography and Reader's Guide to the First Editions of P. G. Wodehouse.* Hamden, CT: Archon Books, 1970.

———. *P. G. Wodehouse: A Portrait of a Master.* London: Garnstone, 1975.

Jeffares, A. Norman. Speech of introduction to the awarding of the doctor of letters degree, Leeds University, 19 May 1960. Burkhart, pp. 17–18.

Johnson, Pamela Hansford. *I. Compton-Burnett.* London: British Council/Longmans, 1951.

Jourdain, M. "I. Compton-Burnett and M. Jourdain: A Conversation." *Orion, A Miscellany,* 1, London: Nicholson and Watson, 1945. Reprint, Burkhart.

Kiely, Robert. *The Romantic Novel in England.* Cambridge: Harvard University Press, 1972.

Kronenberger, Louis. "The Perfect Thriller." *Saturday Review of Literature* (21 June 1947): 9–10 ff. Reprint, as "Max Beerbohm," in Louis Kronenberger, *The Republic of Letters.* New York: Knopf, 1955. Reprint, Riewald.

Liddell, Robert. *A Treatise on the Novel.* London: Jonathan Cape: 1947.

Mayoux, Jean-Jacques. *Un Epicurien Anglais.* Paris: Presses Modernes, 1932.

Mortimer, Raymond. Review of *A House and Its Head* by I. Compton-Burnett. *New Statesman and Nation,* 13 July 1935. Reprint, Burkhart.

Newton, Esther. *Mother Camp: Female Impersonators in America.* Chicago: University of Chicago Press, 1979.

Nicholson, Harold. "*Zuleika Dobson*—a Revaluation." *The Listener* 25 (September 1947): 521–22. Reprint, Riewald.

Orwell, George. *The Collected Essays, Journalism, and Letters of George Orwell.* Edited by Sonia Orwell and Ian Angus. 4 vols. New York: Harcourt, Brace and World, 1968.

Partridge, Eric. "Camp." *A Dictionary of Slang and Unconventional English.* 8th ed. London: Routledge and Kegan Paul, 1984.

Potoker, Edward Martin. *Ronald Firbank.* New York: Columbia University Press, 1969.

Powell, Anthony. Obituary notice for Ivy Compton-Burnett. *Spectator* (6 September 1969): 304. Reprint, Burkhart.

Praz, Mario. "The Novels of Ivy Compton-Burnett." RAI Radio (Televisione Italiana) lecture, 1 April 1955. Reprint, Burkhart.

Priestley, J. B. *Thomas Love Peacock.* Introduction by J. I. M. Stewart. New York: St. Martin's Press, 1966.

Pritchett, V. S. *The Tale Bearers: Literary Essays.* New York: Random House, 1980.

Reavell, Cynthia and Tony. *E. F. Benson: Mr. Benson Remembered in Rye and the World of Tilling.* Rye, England: Martello Bookshop, 1984.

Riewald, J. G. *The Surprise of Excellence: Modern Essays on Max Beerbohm.* Hamden, CT: Archon, 1974.

Rubin, Louis D., Jr. "Susan Sontag and the Camp Followers." *Sewanee Review* 82 (Summer 1974): 503–10.

Rudnick, Paul, and Kurt Anderson. "The Irony Epidemic: How Camp Changed from Lush to Lite." *Spy* (March 1989): 93–98.

Ryan, A. P. "Wooster's Progress." *New Statesman and Nation* (20 June 1953): 737–38.

Sackville-West, Edward. *Inclinations.* London: Seeker and Warburg, 1949.

Sarraute, Nathalie. *The Age of Suspicion.* Translated by Maria Jolas. New York: Braziller, 1963.

Sontag, Susan. "Notes on 'Camp.'" *Partisan Review* (Fall 1964): 515–30. Reprint, *Against Interpretation.* New York: Dell, 1969.

Spedding, James. "Tales by the Author of Headlong Hall." *Edinburgh Review* 68 (January 1839). Reprint, *Peacock: The Satirical Novels: A Casebook.* Edited by Lorna Sage. London: Macmillan, 1976.

Spurling, Hilary. *Ivy: The Life of I. Compton-Burnett.* New York: Knopf, 1984.

Usborne, Richard. *Wodehouse at Work to the End.* London: Barrie and Jenkins, 1976.

———. *A Wodehouse Companion.* London: Hamish Hamilton, 1981.

Viscusi, Robert. *Max Beerbohm; or, The Dandy Dante: Rereading with Mirrors.* Baltimore: Johns Hopkins, 1986.

Ware, J. Redding. *Passing English of the Victorian Age.* New York: Dutton, 1909.

Waugh, Auberon. "Father of the English Idea." *Homage to P. G. Wodehouse.* Edited by Thelma Cazalet-Keir, pp. 137–46.

Waugh, Evelyn. *The Essays, Articles, and Reviews of Evelyn Waugh.* Edited by Donat Gallagher. Boston: Little, Brown, 1984.

White, William. "'Camp' as Adjective: 1909–66." *American Speech: A Quarterly of Linguistic Usage* 41 (1966): 70–72.

Whitt, J. F. *The Strand Magazine 1891–1950: A Selective Checklist Listing All Material Relating to Arthur Conan Doyle, All Stories by P. G. Wodehouse, and a Selection of Other Contributors.* London: J. F. Whitt, 1979.

Wilson, Edmund. "An Analysis of Max Beerbohm." *New Yorker* (1 May 1948): 80–86. Reprint, *Classics and Commercials: A Literary Chronicle of the Forties.* New York: Farrar, Straus, 1950. Reprint, Riewald.

Index